The C# Playbook

Essential Skills and Projects for .NET and Unity Developers

Booker Blunt

Rafael Sanders

Miguel Farmer

Boozman Richard

How to Scan a Barcode to Get a Repository

1. **Install a QR/Barcode Scanner** – Ensure you have a barcode or QR code scanner app installed on your smartphone or use a built-in scanner in **GitHub, GitLab, or Bitbucket.**

2. **Open the Scanner** – Launch the scanner app and grant necessary camera permissions.

3. **Scan the Barcode** – Align the barcode within the scanning frame. The scanner will automatically detect and process it.

4. **Follow the Link** – The scanned result will display a **URL to the repository.** Tap the link to open it in your web browser or Git client.

5. **Clone the Repository** – Use **Git clone** with the provided URL to download the repository to your local machine.

Chapter 1: Introduction to C# and .NET Development

What is C#?

C# (pronounced "C-sharp") is a modern, object-oriented programming language developed by Microsoft. It's the primary language used for developing applications within the .NET framework. Whether you're building web applications, desktop apps, mobile apps, or games, C# provides an incredibly versatile and powerful platform for development.

Real-World Analogy: Think of C# as a Swiss Army knife in the development world. It's a tool that can do everything from cutting a rope to opening a bottle—just like how C# can build everything from small desktop applications to massive, feature-rich web applications.

C# is widely used across industries for building a range of applications, especially in the enterprise sector. The language's syntax is similar to other C-based languages like C++, C, and Java, so if you're familiar with those, you'll pick up C# very quickly.

What is the .NET Framework?

The .NET Framework is a powerful software development platform designed by Microsoft to simplify the development of applications. .NET provides a huge set of libraries, APIs, and tools to help you develop a variety of applications—from web to desktop to mobile—and even for cloud environments.

.NET is a framework that supports multiple programming languages, and C# is one of the primary languages designed to work with .NET. Think of .NET as a giant toolbox where C# is one of the essential tools that you use to build robust applications.

Real-World Analogy: Imagine you're building a house. The .NET framework is the entire construction site, with all the materials and tools, while C# is your hammer, screwdriver, and other tools you use to put things together.

Why Use C# and .NET?

- **Versatility:** From building mobile apps with Xamarin to game development with Unity, C# is used in many domains.
- **Cross-Platform Compatibility:** The introduction of .NET Core allows you to build applications that run on multiple platforms like Windows, macOS, and Linux.
- **Efficiency and Productivity:** With features like garbage collection, easy-to-use libraries, and a vast ecosystem, C# and .NET allow developers to build fast, scalable applications quickly.
- **Strong Community Support:** Microsoft's backing and a strong, growing developer community means a wealth of resources for learning and problem-solving.

Hands-On Project: Hello World in C#

In this project, we'll guide you through creating your first C# application, the "Hello World" program, using Visual Studio.

Step 1: Install Visual Studio

To start coding in C#, you'll need an Integrated Development Environment (IDE). Visual Studio is the most popular IDE for C# development. It's free for students and individual developers through the Visual Studio Community Edition.

1. **Download Visual Studio:** Go to the Visual Studio website, and download the latest version of Visual Studio Community Edition.

2. **Install Visual Studio**: Follow the installation steps. Make sure to select ".NET desktop development" during installation to install the necessary tools for C# development.

Step 2: Create a New Console Application

1. **Open Visual Studio**: Launch Visual Studio after installation.
2. **Create New Project**: Click on "Create a new project."
3. **Select Console Application**: Choose "Console App (.NET Core)" for a simple C# console application.
4. **Name Your Project**: Give your project a name, like "HelloWorld" and click "Create."

Step 3: Write Your Code

Once your project is set up, you'll see a default class named `Program` in the main code editor window. Now, let's write a basic C# program.

```csharp
using System;

namespace HelloWorld
{
    class Program
    {
        static void Main(string[] args)
        {
            Console.WriteLine("Hello, World!");
        }
    }
}
```

- **Using System**: This tells the program that we're going to use the System library, which provides useful classes like `Console`.
- **Namespace**: `HelloWorld` is the namespace, essentially the "folder" that holds your classes.
- **Main Method**: This is where your program starts executing. Every C# program must have a `Main()` method, even if it's just a simple "Hello World."
- **Console.WriteLine**: This is a function that writes text to the console window. In this case, it's displaying "Hello, World!" on the screen.

Step 4: Run Your Application

1. **Run the Program**: Press `Ctrl` + `F5` or click the "Start" button at the top of Visual Studio.
2. **View the Output**: You'll see "Hello, World!" printed in the console window.

Congratulations! You've just created your first C# application.

Key Concepts Covered

Let's break down the key concepts covered in your "Hello World" program:

1. **Variables**: A variable is like a container that holds data. In our example, we didn't explicitly use variables, but in future projects, you'll store data in variables like numbers, strings, etc.
2. **Basic Syntax**: The structure of the code you write—like curly braces `{}`, keywords like `class`, and `static`, and how they come together to make a program work.

3. **Loops**: In more advanced projects, you'll learn about loops, which allow you to repeat actions multiple times without writing the same code over and over.
4. **Conditionals**: These are used to make decisions in your program (for example, "If the user enters a number greater than 10, show this message").

What You'll Need

To follow along with this book, here's a brief list of what you'll need:

Software

- **Visual Studio** (free version available)
    - A powerful IDE for building C# and .NET applications.
- **.NET SDK** (if not included with Visual Studio)
    - The Software Development Kit that enables you to build and run .NET applications.

Hardware

- **A Computer** (Windows, macOS, or Linux)
    - C# and .NET development can be done on any of these operating systems, but Windows is the most common platform for .NET development.
- **Basic Text Editor** (Optional, Visual Studio has this built-in)

Real-World Applications

While creating a "Hello World" program is a simple exercise, C# and .NET are used in some amazing real-world applications:

- **Web Applications**: C# and ASP.NET Core are widely used to build high-performance, scalable web applications.
- **Mobile Applications**: Xamarin, a .NET-based framework, allows you to build cross-platform mobile apps for iOS and Android.
- **Game Development**: Unity, one of the most popular game engines, uses C# as its primary programming language for developing both 2D and 3D games.

Key Concepts Covered in this Chapter

- **Basic Syntax**: How to structure a C# program.
- **Variables**: Storing and manipulating data.
- **Loops**: Repeating tasks efficiently.
- **Conditionals**: Making decisions in code.

Practical, Real-World Example

To make this even more practical, let's take a look at how the skills you've just learned could be used in a real-world application:

Imagine you're tasked with building a basic order-tracking application for a small e-commerce store. You could use C# to:

- Take in user input for new orders.
- Use loops to process a list of orders.
- Use conditionals to determine the shipping method based on the order value.

Conclusion

In this chapter, we introduced you to the C# language and the .NET framework. We also created a basic "Hello World" application using Visual Studio, which introduced key concepts like variables, basic syntax, loops, and conditionals.

By the end of this chapter, you should feel confident in your ability to write basic C# programs. You've also seen how these skills can apply to real-world projects, from web and mobile applications to games and enterprise software.

Chapter 2: Understanding Object-Oriented Programming (OOP) in C#

Introduction to OOP in C#

Object-Oriented Programming (OOP) is a programming paradigm that organizes software design around data, or objects, rather than functions and logic. Objects represent real-world entities, and these objects are instances of **classes**—the blueprints that define what an object will look like and how it behaves.

In C#, OOP helps developers structure code in a more intuitive, reusable, and maintainable way. It divides complex programs into simpler, smaller, and more manageable sections. Let's dive into the core principles of OOP and explore how they work in C#.

Core Principles of OOP

OOP is built on four main principles:

1. **Classes and Objects**
2. **Inheritance**
3. **Polymorphism**
4. **Encapsulation**

1. Classes and Objects

- **Classes**: A class is like a blueprint for creating objects (instances). It defines the properties and methods that its objects will have.
- **Objects**: An object is an instance of a class. It holds real data, like a specific person with a name and age or a product in an inventory.

In simple terms, a **class** is the structure, and an **object** is the living, breathing entity created from that structure.

Example: Imagine a class called `Car`. A `Car` class could have properties like `Make`, `Model`, and `Year`, and methods like `Start()` and `Stop()`. Each individual car object would have specific values for those properties (e.g., `Make` = `"Toyota"`, `Model` = `"Corolla"`, etc.).

Hands-On Example:

```csharp
using System;

namespace OOPExample
{
    class Car
    {
        // Properties
        public string Make;
        public string Model;
        public int Year;

        // Method
        public void Start()
        {
            Console.WriteLine("The car has started.");
```

```
        }
    public void Stop()
    {
        Console.WriteLine("The car has
stopped.");
    }
}

class Program
{
    static void Main(string[] args)
    {
        // Create an object of the Car class
        Car myCar = new Car();
        myCar.Make = "Toyota";
        myCar.Model = "Corolla";
        myCar.Year = 2022;

        Console.WriteLine($"Car: {myCar.Make}
{myCar.Model} ({myCar.Year})");
        myCar.Start();
        myCar.Stop();
    }
}
}
```

In this example:

- The Car class defines properties and methods.
- The myCar object is an instance of the Car class with specific values for Make, Model, and Year.

2. Inheritance

Inheritance allows one class to inherit the properties and methods of another class. It's like a child inheriting traits from their parents, but the child can also add new features or modify existing ones.

Example: Let's say we have a base class `Vehicle`, and we want to create specialized versions of it, like `Car` and `Truck`. Both `Car` and `Truck` should share some properties and methods from `Vehicle`, but they can also have their own specific properties and behaviors.

Hands-On Example:

```csharp
using System;

namespace OOPExample
{
    class Vehicle
    {
        public string Make;
        public string Model;
        public int Year;

        public void Start()
        {
            Console.WriteLine("The vehicle has started.");
        }

        public void Stop()
        {
            Console.WriteLine("The vehicle has stopped.");
        }
    }

    class Car : Vehicle
    {
        public int Doors;

        public void Honk()
        {
            Console.WriteLine("The car is honking.");
        }
    }
```

```
class Truck : Vehicle
{
    public int LoadCapacity;

    public void Haul()
    {
        Console.WriteLine("The truck is hauling a
load.");
    }
}

class Program
{
    static void Main(string[] args)
    {
        Car myCar = new Car();
        myCar.Make = "Toyota";
        myCar.Model = "Camry";
        myCar.Year = 2022;
        myCar.Doors = 4;

        myCar.Start();
        myCar.Honk();

        Truck myTruck = new Truck();
        myTruck.Make = "Ford";
        myTruck.Model = "F-150";
        myTruck.Year = 2022;
        myTruck.LoadCapacity = 1500;

        myTruck.Start();
        myTruck.Haul();
    }
}
}
```

In this example:

- Car and Truck inherit the properties and methods of the Vehicle class.

- They can also have their own additional methods like `Honk` for `Car` and `Haul` for `Truck`.

3. Polymorphism

Polymorphism allows objects of different classes to be treated as objects of a common base class. It also allows you to define methods with the same name in different classes, but each method may behave differently.

Example: In the case of a `Vehicle`, both `Car` and `Truck` might have a method called `Drive`, but the implementation of `Drive` may vary for each type of vehicle.

Hands-On Example:

```csharp
using System;

namespace OOPExample
{
    class Vehicle
    {
        public string Make;
        public string Model;

        public virtual void Drive()
        {
            Console.WriteLine("The vehicle is
driving.");
        }
    }

    class Car : Vehicle
    {
        public int Doors;

        public override void Drive()
        {
```

```
            Console.WriteLine("The car is driving
smoothly.");
        }
    }

    class Truck : Vehicle
    {
        public int LoadCapacity;

        public override void Drive()
        {
            Console.WriteLine("The truck is driving
with a heavy load.");
        }
    }

    class Program
    {
        static void Main(string[] args)
        {
            Vehicle myCar = new Car();
            myCar.Drive();   // Outputs: "The car is
driving smoothly."

            Vehicle myTruck = new Truck();
            myTruck.Drive();   // Outputs: "The truck
is driving with a heavy load."
        }
    }
}
```

In this example:

- The `Drive` method is **overridden** in both the `Car` and `Truck` classes.
- Even though both `Car` and `Truck` are treated as `Vehicle` objects, their specific `Drive` methods behave differently.

4. Encapsulation

Encapsulation refers to the bundling of data (variables) and methods that operate on the data into a single unit or class. It also restricts direct access to some of an object's components and can prevent unintended interference and misuse of the data.

Example: We can use **properties** in C# to encapsulate fields so that they can't be accessed directly but can be modified through methods or properties with **getters** and **setters**.

Hands-On Example:

```csharp
using System;

namespace OOPExample
{
    class Car
    {
        private string make;
        private string model;
        private int year;

        // Property for 'Make'
        public string Make
        {
            get { return make; }
            set { make = value; }
        }

        // Property for 'Model'
        public string Model
        {
            get { return model; }
            set { model = value; }
        }
```

```csharp
        // Property for 'Year'
        public int Year
        {
            get { return year; }
            set
            {
                if (value > 1900 && value < 2100)   //
Validation for year
                {
                    year = value;
                }
                else
                {
                    Console.WriteLine("Invalid
year.");
                }
            }
        }
    }

    class Program
    {
        static void Main(string[] args)
        {
            Car myCar = new Car();
            myCar.Make = "Toyota";
            myCar.Model = "Corolla";
            myCar.Year = 2022;

            Console.WriteLine($"Car: {myCar.Make}
{myCar.Model} ({myCar.Year})");
        }
    }
}
```

In this example:

- The properties Make, Model, and Year encapsulate the fields of the Car class.
- The Year property has a validation check to ensure it is within a valid range.

Hands-On Project: Building an Inventory Management System Using OOP

Now that we have a solid understanding of OOP, let's build a small inventory management system. The system will demonstrate the use of **classes**, **inheritance**, and **polymorphism**.

Step 1: Define the Base Class (`Product`)

csharp

```csharp
class Product
{
    public string Name;
    public decimal Price;
    public int StockQuantity;

    public Product(string name, decimal price, int
stockQuantity)
    {
        Name = name;
```

```
        Price = price;
        StockQuantity = stockQuantity;
    }

    public void DisplayProductInfo()
    {
        Console.WriteLine($"Product: {Name} | Price:
{Price:C} | In Stock: {StockQuantity}");
    }

    public virtual void Sell(int quantity)
    {
        if (StockQuantity >= quantity)
        {
            StockQuantity -= quantity;
            Console.WriteLine($"Sold {quantity}
{Name}(s). Remaining stock: {StockQuantity}");
        }
        else
        {
            Console.WriteLine("Not enough stock.");
        }
    }
}
```

Step 2: Create Subclasses (Electronic and Furniture)

csharp

```
class Electronic : Product
{
    public int WarrantyYears;

    public Electronic(string name, decimal price, int
stockQuantity, int warrantyYears)
        : base(name, price, stockQuantity)
    {
        WarrantyYears = warrantyYears;
    }

    public override void Sell(int quantity)
    {
        base.Sell(quantity);
        Console.WriteLine($"Warranty period:
{WarrantyYears} years.");
```

```csharp
    }
}

class Furniture : Product
{
    public string Material;

    public Furniture(string name, decimal price, int
stockQuantity, string material)
        : base(name, price, stockQuantity)
    {
        Material = material;
    }

    public override void Sell(int quantity)
    {
        base.Sell(quantity);
        Console.WriteLine($"Material: {Material}");
    }
}
```

Step 3: Implement the Inventory Management System

csharp

```csharp
class Inventory
{
    private List<Product> products = new
List<Product>();

    public void AddProduct(Product product)
    {
        products.Add(product);
    }

    public void ShowInventory()
    {
        foreach (var product in products)
        {
            product.DisplayProductInfo();
        }
    }
}
```

Step 4: Use the Inventory System in the Main Program

csharp

```csharp
class Program
{
    static void Main(string[] args)
    {
        Inventory inventory = new Inventory();

        // Add products to inventory
        inventory.AddProduct(new Electronic("Laptop",
1200.99m, 10, 2));
        inventory.AddProduct(new Furniture("Chair",
59.99m, 20, "Wood"));

        // Display inventory
        inventory.ShowInventory();

        // Sell a product
        inventory.SellProduct("Laptop", 2);
    }
}
```

Conclusion

In this chapter, we've covered the key principles of Object-Oriented Programming (OOP) in C#: classes, objects, inheritance, polymorphism, and encapsulation. Using hands-on examples, we built a simple inventory management system, applying these principles to create a reusable, extensible code structure.

By now, you should have a solid understanding of how OOP helps in structuring complex systems and making code more maintainable and scalable. In the next chapter, we'll dive deeper into more advanced C# features like **LINQ** and **delegates**. Stay tuned!

Chapter 3: Mastering Collections, Lists, and Arrays

Introduction to Collections, Lists, and Arrays

In this chapter, we'll explore one of the most powerful and useful concepts in programming: collections. Collections allow you to store and manipulate large amounts of data in an organized way. In C#, collections come in many different forms, including arrays, lists, dictionaries, and sets, each with its own unique properties and use cases.

The goal of this chapter is to give you a deep understanding of how these collections work, how to use them effectively, and how to leverage their power in your own projects. By the end of this chapter, you'll be comfortable using these data structures to tackle real-world problems like building a **contacts manager**—a project that will allow you to add, update, and delete contact information using collections.

What Are Collections?

At its core, a **collection** is any data structure that holds a group of related objects. These objects can be of the same or different types, depending on the type of collection you use. Collections provide you with powerful tools to organize and manipulate data, which is essential for building more efficient and scalable software.

In this chapter, we'll dive into:

- **Arrays**: Fixed-size collections of elements.
- **Lists**: Dynamic arrays that grow as needed.
- **Dictionaries**: Collections of key-value pairs.
- **Sets**: Collections of unique elements.

Each of these collections will be covered in detail, and we'll see how they can be used in practical applications.

What You'll Need

Before we dive into the hands-on project, let's ensure that you have the tools needed to follow along:

Software Requirements:

- **Visual Studio**: This is the most popular Integrated Development Environment (IDE) for C# development. Visual Studio provides a user-friendly interface to write, test, and debug C# code. It also includes support for .NET Core and other useful frameworks.
    - o **Download**: You can download Visual Studio Community Edition for free from Visual Studio's website.
- **.NET SDK**: The Software Development Kit (SDK) is required to build and run .NET Core applications. Visual Studio typically includes this during installation, but you can install it separately if needed.
- **Operating System**: Windows, macOS, or Linux. The examples in this chapter are cross-platform, and you'll be able to run them on any of these operating systems.

Hardware Requirements:

- A basic computer or laptop with at least 4GB of RAM should be sufficient for running Visual Studio and coding in C#.

Prerequisites:

- Basic knowledge of C# syntax (variables, loops, and conditional statements). If you haven't gone through the previous chapters, it's a good idea to familiarize yourself with the basics before proceeding.

Chapter Outline

1. Introduction to Arrays

An **array** is a collection of elements, all of which are of the same type. The elements are stored in contiguous memory locations, making it easy to access elements by their index (position). Arrays are fixed in size, meaning once you create them, the number of elements they can hold cannot be changed.

Creating and Using Arrays

Let's start with a simple array example where we create an array of integers and iterate through it.

```csharp
using System;

class Program
{
    static void Main(string[] args)
    {
        // Create an array of integers
        int[] numbers = { 1, 2, 3, 4, 5 };

        // Loop through the array and print each number
        foreach (int number in numbers)
        {
            Console.WriteLine(number);
        }
    }
}
```

Explanation:

- We created an array called `numbers` that holds five integers.
- The `foreach` loop is used to iterate over each element in the array and print it to the console.

Limitations of Arrays

Arrays have a fixed size, so if you need to add or remove elements dynamically, arrays may not be the best option. We will cover dynamic collections like lists later in this chapter.

---

2. Mastering Lists

A **list** is similar to an array but has the advantage of being dynamic, meaning it can grow or shrink in size as needed. Lists are part of the `System.Collections.Generic` namespace in C#, and they provide more flexibility than arrays.

Creating and Using Lists

Here's an example of how you can use a list to store and manipulate data dynamically.

```csharp
using System;
using System.Collections.Generic;

class Program
{
    static void Main(string[] args)
    {
        // Create a list of strings
        List<string> contacts = new List<string>();

        // Add items to the list
```

```
contacts.Add("John Doe");
contacts.Add("Jane Smith");
contacts.Add("Samuel Johnson");

// Display the contacts
foreach (string contact in contacts)
{
    Console.WriteLine(contact);
}

// Remove an item from the list
contacts.Remove("Jane Smith");

// Display updated list
Console.WriteLine("\nAfter removal:");
foreach (string contact in contacts)
{
    Console.WriteLine(contact);
}
    }
}
```

Explanation:

- We created a list of strings called `contacts` to store contact names.
- We added items to the list using `Add()`, then displayed them with a `foreach` loop.
- We removed an item from the list with the `Remove()` method, and then displayed the updated list.

When to Use Lists

- **Dynamic Size**: Lists are ideal when you don't know in advance how many elements you'll need to store.
- **Performance**: Lists are optimized for adding, removing, and accessing elements.

3. Exploring Dictionaries

A **dictionary** is a collection of key-value pairs. Each item in a dictionary is identified by a unique key, and you can retrieve or modify the value associated with that key.

Creating and Using Dictionaries

Let's create a contacts manager where each contact has a unique ID. We will use a dictionary to store the contacts.

```csharp
using System;
using System.Collections.Generic;

class Program
{
    static void Main(string[] args)
    {
        // Create a dictionary to store contacts
        Dictionary<int, string> contacts = new
Dictionary<int, string>();

        // Add contacts with unique IDs
        contacts.Add(1, "John Doe");
        contacts.Add(2, "Jane Smith");
        contacts.Add(3, "Samuel Johnson");

        // Display contacts
        foreach (KeyValuePair<int, string> contact in
contacts)
        {
            Console.WriteLine($"ID: {contact.Key},
Name: {contact.Value}");
        }

        // Remove a contact by ID
        contacts.Remove(2);

        // Display updated contacts
```

```
        Console.WriteLine("\nAfter removal:");
        foreach (KeyValuePair<int, string> contact in
contacts)
        {
            Console.WriteLine($"ID: {contact.Key},
Name: {contact.Value}");
        }
    }
}
```

Explanation:

- We created a dictionary where the key is an integer (representing the contact ID) and the value is a string (the contact's name).
- We used `Add()` to add contacts, and `Remove()` to delete a contact by its key.

When to Use Dictionaries

- **Key-Value Pairs**: Dictionaries are great when you need to associate a unique key with a value (e.g., looking up contact names by their unique IDs).
- **Fast Lookups**: Dictionaries provide efficient lookup times for retrieving values using keys.

4. Using Sets

A **set** is a collection of unique elements. Sets do not allow duplicates and are useful when you need to ensure that each element appears only once.

Creating and Using Sets

In this example, let's create a set of phone numbers. We'll add some numbers to the set and then display them.

```csharp
using System;
using System.Collections.Generic;

class Program
{
    static void Main(string[] args)
    {
        // Create a set of phone numbers
        HashSet<string> phoneNumbers = new
HashSet<string>();

        // Add phone numbers to the set
        phoneNumbers.Add("555-1234");
        phoneNumbers.Add("555-5678");
        phoneNumbers.Add("555-1234"); // Duplicate,
won't be added

        // Display the phone numbers
        foreach (string number in phoneNumbers)
        {
            Console.WriteLine(number);
        }
    }
}
```

Explanation:

- We created a `HashSet` to store phone numbers.
- When we tried to add the duplicate phone number `"555-1234"`, it was not added to the set since sets do not allow duplicates.

When to Use Sets

- **Uniqueness**: Use sets when you need to store unique items and don't want duplicates.
- **Efficient Lookup**: Sets provide fast lookups and are efficient when dealing with large collections.

Hands-On Project: Contacts Manager

Now that we've explored arrays, lists, dictionaries, and sets, let's build a contacts manager that allows adding, updating, and deleting contact information using collections.

We will use **a dictionary** to store contact information, where each contact has a unique ID.

Step 1: Define the Contact Class
csharp

```csharp
using System;
using System.Collections.Generic;

class Contact
{
    public int ID { get; set; }
    public string Name { get; set; }
    public string PhoneNumber { get; set; }

    public Contact(int id, string name, string
phoneNumber)
    {
        ID = id;
        Name = name;
        PhoneNumber = phoneNumber;
    }
}
```

Step 2: Implement the Contacts Manager

csharp

```csharp
class ContactsManager
{
    private Dictionary<int, Contact> contacts = new
Dictionary<int, Contact>();

    public void AddContact(Contact contact)
    {
        if (!contacts.ContainsKey(contact.ID))
        {
            contacts.Add(contact.ID, contact);
            Console.WriteLine("Contact added.");
        }
        else
        {
            Console.WriteLine("Contact with this ID
already exists.");
        }
    }

    public void UpdateContact(int id, string newName,
string newPhoneNumber)
    {
        if (contacts.ContainsKey(id))
        {
            contacts[id].Name = newName;
            contacts[id].PhoneNumber =
newPhoneNumber;
            Console.WriteLine("Contact updated.");
        }
        else
        {
            Console.WriteLine("Contact not found.");
        }
    }

    public void DeleteContact(int id)
    {
        if (contacts.ContainsKey(id))
        {
            contacts.Remove(id);
            Console.WriteLine("Contact deleted.");
```

```csharp
        }
        else
        {
            Console.WriteLine("Contact not found.");
        }
    }

    public void ShowContacts()
    {
        foreach (var contact in contacts)
        {
            Console.WriteLine($"ID:
{contact.Value.ID}, Name: {contact.Value.Name},
Phone: {contact.Value.PhoneNumber}");
        }
    }
}
```

Step 3: Use the Contacts Manager in the Main Program

csharp

```csharp
class Program
{
    static void Main(string[] args)
    {
        ContactsManager manager = new
ContactsManager();

        // Adding contacts
        manager.AddContact(new Contact(1, "John Doe",
"555-1234"));
        manager.AddContact(new Contact(2, "Jane
Smith", "555-5678"));

        // Displaying contacts
        manager.ShowContacts();

        // Updating a contact
        manager.UpdateContact(1, "John Doe", "555-
4321");

        // Deleting a contact
        manager.DeleteContact(2);
```

```
        // Displaying updated contacts
        manager.ShowContacts();
    }
}
```

Conclusion

In this chapter, we covered the basics of **collections** in C#—arrays, lists, dictionaries, and sets—along with practical examples for using each one. We built a contacts manager project that demonstrated the use of **a dictionary** to store and manipulate contact data. With hands-on practice, you've learned how to add, update, and delete data in collections, a key skill for building real-world applications.

Next, we'll dive deeper into more advanced topics like **LINQ** and **delegates**. Keep practicing, and you'll soon be able to build even more powerful applications using C# collections!

Chapter 4: C# LINQ: Simplifying Data Operations

Introduction to LINQ

In this chapter, we'll introduce you to one of the most powerful features in C#: **Language Integrated Query** (LINQ). LINQ allows developers to query data from different data sources—arrays, lists, databases, XML files, and more—directly within C#. It provides a simple and readable syntax for performing common operations like filtering, sorting, and transforming data, all without needing to write complex code.

The beauty of LINQ lies in its ability to allow developers to work with data in a way that is integrated into the C# language itself. In the past, working with data in C# often required writing verbose and complex loops or using external libraries. LINQ revolutionizes that by simplifying these operations, enabling faster, more readable, and maintainable code.

Throughout this chapter, we'll explore the key features of LINQ, walk through real-world examples, and provide a hands-on project to help solidify your understanding of LINQ's capabilities.

What Is LINQ?

Language Integrated Query (LINQ) is a set of methods in C# that provide a uniform, query-based approach to retrieving and manipulating data. It enables you to use the C# language to query various data sources like:

- **Arrays and Collections**: Arrays, Lists, Dictionaries
- **Databases**: SQL databases (via LINQ to SQL)
- **XML**: XML documents
- **Web Services**: Data from web services

In essence, LINQ allows you to **write SQL-like queries** directly in C# syntax.

Key Benefits of LINQ:

- **Concise and Readable**: LINQ reduces the amount of boilerplate code required to manipulate data.
- **Strongly Typed**: LINQ ensures that your queries are type-safe at compile time, reducing runtime errors.
- **Intuitive Syntax**: LINQ queries are written using C# syntax, which makes them easier to read and maintain.
- **Cross-Source Queries**: With LINQ, you can easily query data from multiple sources, such as a list and a database, in a unified way.

Types of LINQ Queries

There are two ways to write LINQ queries in C#:

1. **Query Syntax**: A SQL-like syntax that is more readable and declarative.

2. **Method Syntax**: A fluent API style syntax that uses extension methods for more flexibility and control.

What You'll Need

Before we dive into LINQ queries, let's ensure that you have everything set up to follow along with this chapter.

Software Requirements:

- **Visual Studio**: We'll be using Visual Studio as our Integrated Development Environment (IDE) to write and execute C# code. It provides excellent support for LINQ and C# in general.
    - o **Download**: Visual Studio Community Edition can be downloaded from Visual Studio's website.
- **.NET SDK**: LINQ is part of the .NET Core framework, so make sure you have the .NET SDK installed to build and run your C# projects.

Hardware Requirements:

- **A Computer** with at least 4GB of RAM is recommended for running Visual Studio smoothly.

Prerequisites:

- **Basic Knowledge of C# Syntax**: Before diving into LINQ, ensure you're comfortable with basic C# concepts such as loops, arrays, and lists. If you're new to C#, the previous chapters will provide a strong foundation for understanding LINQ.

- **Basic Understanding of Data Structures**: Familiarity with arrays, lists, and dictionaries will be helpful as we work with data structures in this chapter.

1. Basic LINQ Operations: Filtering, Sorting, and Searching

We'll start by exploring the fundamental LINQ operations that you'll use regularly in your applications: **filtering**, **sorting**, and **searching**.

Filtering Data Using LINQ

Let's begin with a basic LINQ query to filter data. For example, let's create a list of employees and filter out those whose salary is above a certain threshold.

```csharp
using System;
using System.Collections.Generic;
using System.Linq;

class Program
{
    static void Main(string[] args)
    {
        // Create a list of employees
        List<Employee> employees = new List<Employee>
        {
            new Employee { Id = 1, Name = "John Doe",
Salary = 50000 },
            new Employee { Id = 2, Name = "Jane
Smith", Salary = 60000 },
```

```
            new Employee { Id = 3, Name = "Samuel
Johnson", Salary = 40000 },
            new Employee { Id = 4, Name = "Martha
Davis", Salary = 70000 }
        };

        // LINQ query to filter employees with a
salary greater than 50,000
        var highEarners = from emp in employees
                          where emp.Salary > 50000
                          select emp;

        // Display filtered results
        foreach (var emp in highEarners)
        {
            Console.WriteLine($"{emp.Name} earns
{emp.Salary:C}");
        }
    }
}

public class Employee
{
    public int Id { get; set; }
    public string Name { get; set; }
    public double Salary { get; set; }
}
```

Explanation:

- We created a list of employees, each with an Id, Name, and Salary.
- The LINQ query filters the employees where the salary is greater than 50,000. This is a basic **filtering** operation using the where clause.

Sorting Data Using LINQ

Now, let's see how to **sort** data using LINQ. We'll sort the employees by salary in ascending and descending order.

```csharp
// Sort employees by salary in ascending order
var sortedEmployees = from emp in employees
                      orderby emp.Salary ascending
                      select emp;

// Display sorted results
foreach (var emp in sortedEmployees)
{
    Console.WriteLine($"{emp.Name} earns
{emp.Salary:C}");
}
```

Explanation:

- The `orderby` clause allows us to sort the employees by salary. In this case, we're sorting in **ascending** order.

For descending order:

```csharp
// Sort employees by salary in descending order
var sortedEmployeesDesc = from emp in employees
                          orderby emp.Salary
descending
                          select emp;
```

Searching Data Using LINQ

Searching is another common operation. Let's search for an employee by their name using LINQ.

```csharp
// Search for an employee named "Jane Smith"
var employeeSearch = employees.FirstOrDefault(e =>
e.Name == "Jane Smith");

if (employeeSearch != null)
```

```
{
    Console.WriteLine($"{employeeSearch.Name} found
with salary {employeeSearch.Salary:C}");
}
else
{
    Console.WriteLine("Employee not found.");
}
```

Explanation:

- `FirstOrDefault()` searches the collection and returns the first employee that matches the condition. If no match is found, it returns `null`.

2. Advanced LINQ Operations: Grouping, Aggregation, and Joins

Now that we've covered basic LINQ operations, let's move on to more advanced features, including **grouping, aggregation**, and **joining** data from multiple sources.

Grouping Data Using LINQ

Grouping data is useful when you need to categorize items based on a specific attribute. In this example, we'll group employees by their salary ranges.

csharp

```
// Group employees by salary range
var groupedBySalary = from emp in employees
                      group emp by emp.Salary >=
60000 ? "High Earners" : "Low Earners" into
salaryGroup
                      select salaryGroup;
```

```
foreach (var group in groupedBySalary)
{
    Console.WriteLine($"{group.Key}:");
    foreach (var emp in group)
    {
        Console.WriteLine($"  {emp.Name},
{emp.Salary:C}");
    }
}
```

Explanation:

- We used the `group by` clause to categorize employees into two groups: "High Earners" and "Low Earners" based on their salary.
- This allows us to **group** data dynamically within the LINQ query.

Aggregating Data Using LINQ

Aggregation operations like **sum, average,** and **count** are commonly used to calculate summary statistics from a collection.

csharp

```
// Calculate total salary of all employees
double totalSalary = employees.Sum(emp =>
emp.Salary);
Console.WriteLine($"Total salary: {totalSalary:C}");

// Calculate average salary
double averageSalary = employees.Average(emp =>
emp.Salary);
Console.WriteLine($"Average salary:
{averageSalary:C}");
```

Explanation:

- `Sum()` calculates the total salary of all employees.
- `Average()` calculates the average salary of all employees.

Joining Data Using LINQ

Let's now see how to join two collections using LINQ. We'll join an employee list with a department list to get the department for each employee.

csharp

```
using System;
using System.Collections.Generic;
using System.Linq;

class Program
{
    static void Main(string[] args)
    {
        List<Employee> employees = new List<Employee>
        {
            new Employee { Id = 1, Name = "John Doe",
Salary = 50000, DepartmentId = 1 },
            new Employee { Id = 2, Name = "Jane
Smith", Salary = 60000, DepartmentId = 2 },
            new Employee { Id = 3, Name = "Samuel
Johnson", Salary = 40000, DepartmentId = 1 },
        };

        List<Department> departments = new
List<Department>
        {
            new Department { Id = 1, Name = "Sales"
},
            new Department { Id = 2, Name = "HR" },
        };

        var employeeDepartments = from emp in
employees
```

```
                          join dept in
departments on emp.DepartmentId equals dept.Id
                         select new {
emp.Name, emp.Salary, dept.Name };

        foreach (var item in employeeDepartments)
        {
            Console.WriteLine($"{item.Name} works in
{item.Name} with a salary of {item.Salary:C}");
        }
    }
}

public class Employee
{
    public int Id { get; set; }
    public string Name { get; set; }
    public double Salary { get; set; }
    public int DepartmentId { get; set; }
}

public class Department
{
    public int Id { get; set; }
    public string Name { get; set; }
}
```

Explanation:

- This example demonstrates how to use the `join` keyword to combine data from two collections based on a common field (`DepartmentId` in this case).
- The result is a list of employees with their corresponding department names.

3. Hands-On Project: Employee Contacts Manager

In this project, we'll build a **contacts manager** that can add, update, delete, and search employee records using LINQ to filter and query the data.

Step 1: Define the Employee Class
csharp

```csharp
public class Employee
{
    public int Id { get; set; }
    public string Name { get; set; }
    public double Salary { get; set; }
    public string Department { get; set; }
}
```

Step 2: Create the Employee Manager Class
csharp

```csharp
public class EmployeeManager
{
    private List<Employee> employees = new
List<Employee>();

    public void AddEmployee(Employee employee)
    {
        employees.Add(employee);
    }

    public void UpdateEmployee(int id, string
newName, double newSalary, string newDepartment)
    {
        var employee = employees.FirstOrDefault(emp
=> emp.Id == id);
        if (employee != null)
        {
            employee.Name = newName;
            employee.Salary = newSalary;
```

```csharp
            employee.Department = newDepartment;
        }
    }

    public void DeleteEmployee(int id)
    {
        var employee = employees.FirstOrDefault(emp
=> emp.Id == id);
        if (employee != null)
        {
            employees.Remove(employee);
        }
    }

    public void DisplayEmployees()
    {
        var employeeList = from emp in employees
                           orderby emp.Salary
descending
                           select emp;

        foreach (var emp in employeeList)
        {
            Console.WriteLine($"ID: {emp.Id}, Name:
{emp.Name}, Salary: {emp.Salary:C}, Department:
{emp.Department}");
        }
    }
}
```

Step 3: Implement the Main Program

csharp

```csharp
class Program
{
    static void Main(string[] args)
    {
        EmployeeManager manager = new
EmployeeManager();

        // Adding employees
        manager.AddEmployee(new Employee { Id = 1,
Name = "John Doe", Salary = 50000, Department =
"Sales" });
```

```
        manager.AddEmployee(new Employee { Id = 2,
Name = "Jane Smith", Salary = 60000, Department =
"HR" });

        // Displaying employees
        Console.WriteLine("Employees:");
        manager.DisplayEmployees();

        // Updating an employee
        manager.UpdateEmployee(1, "John Doe", 55000,
"Sales");

        // Deleting an employee
        manager.DeleteEmployee(2);

        // Displaying updated employees
        Console.WriteLine("\nUpdated Employees:");
        manager.DisplayEmployees();
    }
}
```

Conclusion

In this chapter, we've explored the power of **LINQ** for simplifying data operations in C#. We've covered how to filter, sort, and search data with LINQ queries and dived deeper into advanced operations like grouping, aggregation, and joins.

We also completed a hands-on project, building an **Employee Manager** that uses LINQ to manage employee records. As you move forward, you'll find that LINQ is a critical tool for working with large datasets in both small and enterprise-level applications.

In the next chapter, we'll explore **delegates** and **events**, taking your C# skills to the next level. Keep practicing and experimenting with LINQ—it's an invaluable tool for any C# developer!

Chapter 5: Building Applications with .NET Core

Introduction to .NET Core

Welcome to one of the most exciting chapters in your journey as a .NET developer! In this chapter, we will dive into building **cross-platform applications** using **.NET Core**, one of the most powerful frameworks available today. Whether you are developing web applications, APIs, microservices, or business applications, .NET Core provides an open-source, high-performance platform that works on Windows, macOS, and Linux.

The ability to build applications that run anywhere—regardless of operating system—makes .NET Core an excellent choice for modern development. In this chapter, we will cover the essentials of building cross-platform applications using .NET Core, and you will also build your first **CRUD (Create, Read, Update, Delete)** web application using **ASP.NET Core**.

Let's dive in!

What You'll Need

Software Requirements:

- **Visual Studio 2019/2022**: The integrated development environment (IDE) for writing, debugging, and running your .NET Core applications.
  - ○ **Download**: Visual Studio Community Edition is free and can be downloaded from Visual Studio's website.
  - ○ **Important**: During installation, make sure to select the **ASP.NET and web development** workload to install the necessary components for web application development.
- **.NET SDK**: The .NET Core Software Development Kit (SDK) contains the tools necessary to develop .NET Core applications.
  - ○ You can install the .NET SDK from Microsoft's official .NET page.
- **PostgreSQL, MySQL, or SQL Server** (optional): You'll need a database management system (DBMS) for storing data. You can use a local or cloud database, but for simplicity, we will use **SQLite** for the hands-on project in this chapter.
- **Browser**: Any modern web browser (Google Chrome, Firefox, or Edge) to view your application.

Hardware Requirements:

- A computer or laptop with at least **4GB of RAM** should be sufficient for this chapter.

Prerequisites:

- **Basic C# Knowledge**: You should be comfortable with the basics of C# and object-oriented programming.
- **Basic Understanding of Web Development**: Familiarity with concepts like HTTP requests, RESTful APIs, and basic HTML will be helpful.
- **Basic Database Knowledge**: Understanding basic database operations like CRUD will be beneficial but not required.

Chapter Overview

In this chapter, we will walk through the process of building a CRUD web application using **ASP.NET Core**. This web application will simulate a basic **inventory management system**, allowing us to:

1. **Create** new inventory items (products).
2. **Read** the inventory list.
3. **Update** product details.
4. **Delete** products from the inventory.

Getting Started with .NET Core

What is .NET Core?

.NET Core is a cross-platform, open-source framework developed by Microsoft. It is optimized for building modern, cloud-based, high-performance applications. .NET Core runs on multiple platforms, including Windows, macOS, and Linux, and is a great choice for building web applications, APIs, microservices, and console apps.

Key Features of .NET Core:

- **Cross-Platform**: .NET Core runs on Windows, macOS, and Linux.
- **High Performance**: Designed for building high-performance, scalable applications.
- **Open Source**: .NET Core is open source, meaning you can contribute to its development or customize it to suit your needs.
- **Flexible Deployment**: You can deploy .NET Core applications on cloud platforms like Azure, AWS, or on-premises servers.

Setting Up Your Development Environment

Before we start building our application, let's make sure everything is set up correctly. Follow these steps:

1. Install Visual Studio:

If you haven't already, download and install **Visual Studio** Community Edition. Make sure to install the **ASP.NET and web development** workload during installation.

2. Install .NET SDK:

The .NET SDK is required to develop and run .NET Core applications. If you don't have it yet, download the SDK from Microsoft's official .NET page.

3. Set Up the Database:

For simplicity, we will use **SQLite** for the database. SQLite is a lightweight, self-contained database engine that is easy to set up.

You can install **SQLite** via NuGet in your project. If you choose to use a different database like SQL Server or PostgreSQL, the steps will be very similar, but you'll need to modify your connection strings accordingly.

Building the CRUD Application: Step-by-Step

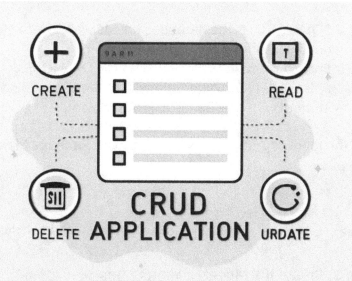

Step 1: Create a New ASP.NET Core Web Application

1. **Open Visual Studio** and create a new project.
2. Select **ASP.NET Core Web Application** and click **Next**.

3. Name your project (e.g., `InventoryApp`) and click **Create**.
4. In the next screen, choose **Web Application (Model-View-Controller)**, which sets up a basic MVC (Model-View-Controller) architecture. Click **Create**.

Your new project will be created with some default files like `Startup.cs`, `Program.cs`, and `appsettings.json`, along with a sample controller and view.

Step 2: Install Necessary Packages

We'll need to install a few NuGet packages to work with SQLite and Entity Framework Core.

1. **SQLite:** This is the database engine we'll use to store our inventory data.
2. **Entity Framework Core:** This is the ORM (Object-Relational Mapping) framework that makes it easy to interact with databases using C# objects.

Run the following commands in the **NuGet Package Manager Console**:

bash

```
Install-Package Microsoft.EntityFrameworkCore.Sqlite
Install-Package Microsoft.EntityFrameworkCore.Tools
```

Step 3: Create the Model (Inventory Item)

In the **Models** folder, create a new class called `InventoryItem.cs`:

csharp

```
using System;

namespace InventoryApp.Models
{
    public class InventoryItem
    {
        public int Id { get; set; }
        public string Name { get; set; }
        public int Quantity { get; set; }
        public decimal Price { get; set; }
    }
}
```

This class represents an inventory item, with properties for the item's `Id`, `Name`, `Quantity`, and `Price`.

Step 4: Create the Database Context

Next, create a database context class that will handle the connection to the SQLite database. Create a new file in the **Data** folder called `ApplicationDbContext.cs`:

csharp

```
using Microsoft.EntityFrameworkCore;
using InventoryApp.Models;

namespace InventoryApp.Data
{
    public class ApplicationDbContext : DbContext
    {
        public
ApplicationDbContext(DbContextOptions<ApplicationDbContext> options)
            : base(options)
        {
        }

        public DbSet<InventoryItem> InventoryItems { get; set; }
    }
```

```
}
```

The `DbContext` class is used to interact with the database. In this case, we are defining a **DbSet** for `InventoryItem`, which will represent the collection of inventory items in the database.

Step 5: Configure the Database Connection

Now, let's configure the connection to our SQLite database. Open the `appsettings.json` file and add the following connection string:

json

```json
{
  "ConnectionStrings": {
    "DefaultConnection": "Data Source=inventory.db"
  }
}
```

This connection string tells Entity Framework to use a SQLite database file called `inventory.db` in the root of the project.

Next, open the `Startup.cs` file and modify the `ConfigureServices` method to use the `ApplicationDbContext`:

csharp

```csharp
public void ConfigureServices(IServiceCollection services)
{

services.AddDbContext<ApplicationDbContext>(options =>

options.UseSqlite(Configuration.GetConnectionString("DefaultConnection")));
```

```
        services.AddControllersWithViews();
}
```

Step 6: Create the Controller

Now, let's create a controller to handle the CRUD operations. In the **Controllers** folder, create a new controller called InventoryController.cs:

csharp

```csharp
using System.Linq;
using Microsoft.AspNetCore.Mvc;
using InventoryApp.Data;
using InventoryApp.Models;

namespace InventoryApp.Controllers
{
    public class InventoryController : Controller
    {
        private readonly ApplicationDbContext _context;

        public InventoryController(ApplicationDbContext context)
        {
            _context = context;
        }

        // GET: Inventory
        public IActionResult Index()
        {
            var items = _context.InventoryItems.ToList();
            return View(items);
        }

        // GET: Inventory/Create
        public IActionResult Create()
        {
            return View();
        }
```

```csharp
        // POST: Inventory/Create
        [HttpPost]
        [ValidateAntiForgeryToken]
        public IActionResult
Create([Bind("Name,Quantity,Price")] InventoryItem
item)
        {
            if (ModelState.IsValid)
            {
                _context.Add(item);
                _context.SaveChanges();
                return
RedirectToAction(nameof(Index));
            }
            return View(item);
        }

        // GET: Inventory/Edit/5
        public IActionResult Edit(int? id)
        {
            if (id == null)
            {
                return NotFound();
            }

            var item =
_context.InventoryItems.Find(id);
            if (item == null)
            {
                return NotFound();
            }
            return View(item);
        }

        // POST: Inventory/Edit/5
        [HttpPost]
        [ValidateAntiForgeryToken]
        public IActionResult Edit(int id,
[Bind("Id,Name,Quantity,Price")] InventoryItem item)
        {
            if (id != item.Id)
            {
                return NotFound();
            }
```

```csharp
            if (ModelState.IsValid)
            {
                try
                {
                    _context.Update(item);
                    _context.SaveChanges();
                }
                catch (DbUpdateConcurrencyException)
                {
                    if
(!InventoryItemExists(item.Id))
                    {
                        return NotFound();
                    }
                    else
                    {
                        throw;
                    }
                }
                return
RedirectToAction(nameof(Index));
            }
            return View(item);
        }

        // GET: Inventory/Delete/5
        public IActionResult Delete(int? id)
        {
            if (id == null)
            {
                return NotFound();
            }

            var item = _context.InventoryItems
                .FirstOrDefault(m => m.Id == id);
            if (item == null)
            {
                return NotFound();
            }

            return View(item);
        }
```

```
// POST: Inventory/Delete/5
[HttpPost, ActionName("Delete")]
[ValidateAntiForgeryToken]
public IActionResult DeleteConfirmed(int id)
{
        var item =
_context.InventoryItems.Find(id);
        _context.InventoryItems.Remove(item);
        _context.SaveChanges();
        return RedirectToAction(nameof(Index));
}

private bool InventoryItemExists(int id)
{
        return _context.InventoryItems.Any(e =>
e.Id == id);
}
    }
}
```

This controller contains actions for each CRUD operation:

- **Index**: Displays the list of inventory items.
- **Create**: Allows users to create new inventory items.
- **Edit**: Allows users to edit existing inventory items.
- **Delete**: Allows users to delete inventory items.

Step 7: Create Views for CRUD Operations

Now, let's create the views for displaying and interacting with inventory items. In the **Views/Inventory** folder, create the following views:

1. **Index.cshtml**: Displays the list of inventory items.
2. **Create.cshtml**: Displays the form for creating a new item.
3. **Edit.cshtml**: Displays the form for editing an existing item.

4. **Delete.cshtml**: Confirms deletion of an item.

These views will allow users to interact with the application through the web interface.

Conclusion

In this chapter, we built a simple **CRUD web application** using **ASP.NET Core** and **SQLite**. By following along with the hands-on examples, you learned how to:

1. Set up an ASP.NET Core web application.
2. Use **Entity Framework Core** to interact with a database.
3. Build the necessary logic for **Create**, **Read**, **Update**, and **Delete** operations in a web application.

This is just the beginning. With these foundations, you can extend this application with advanced features, improve the UI, and integrate other business logic.

Chapter 6: Unit Testing in C#

Introduction to Unit Testing

In the fast-paced world of software development, one of the most critical practices for ensuring code quality and reliability is **unit testing**. Unit tests are a cornerstone of professional software development, allowing developers to catch bugs early, verify that code is working as expected, and maintain the integrity of the software as it evolves.

In this chapter, we will cover the essentials of **unit testing** in **C#**, why it's crucial for professional development, and how it helps to ensure the stability and functionality of business-critical applications. We'll also walk through a hands-on project where you'll write unit tests for a function that calculates the tax for an order in an e-commerce application.

By the end of this chapter, you'll be comfortable writing and running unit tests in C#, and you'll understand how they contribute to the robustness of your code.

What You'll Need

Software Requirements:

1. **Visual Studio:**

- o Visual Studio is the most popular IDE for C# development. It provides built-in support for writing, debugging, and running unit tests.
- o **Download**: You can download Visual Studio Community Edition for free from Visual Studio's website.

2. **.NET SDK:**
   - o The .NET SDK is required to develop and run .NET Core applications, which include unit testing.
   - o Download the .NET SDK from the official .NET page.

3. **Unit Testing Framework:**
   - o **xUnit, NUnit,** or **MSTest** are the most commonly used testing frameworks in C#. In this chapter, we will use **xUnit**, a popular testing framework that is widely adopted in the .NET ecosystem.
   - o You can install **xUnit** via NuGet in Visual Studio.

Hardware Requirements:

- A computer or laptop with **4GB of RAM** should be sufficient for running Visual Studio and writing unit tests.

Prerequisites:

- **Basic Knowledge of C#**: You should be comfortable with C# syntax, basic programming concepts, and object-oriented programming (OOP).
- **Understanding of Functions and Methods**: This chapter will require an understanding of functions, parameters, and return types, as we will write tests for functions.

Chapter Overview

In this chapter, we will:

1. **Understand Unit Testing**: Explore what unit testing is, why it's important, and the benefits it brings to software development.
2. **Write Unit Tests in C#**: Learn how to write unit tests in C# using **xUnit**.
3. **Test a Business Function**: Implement a hands-on project where we write tests for a function that calculates tax for an order in an e-commerce application.
4. **Real-World Applications**: See how unit tests ensure the reliability and correctness of business-critical applications.

What is Unit Testing?

Unit testing refers to the practice of testing individual units or components of a software system to ensure that they work as expected. A **unit** typically refers to a single function or method within your code. Unit testing involves writing small, focused tests that validate the behavior of these units.

Why Unit Testing is Important:

- **Catches Bugs Early**: Unit tests help identify issues at an early stage in the development process, reducing the likelihood of bugs making it to production.

- **Improves Code Quality**: Writing tests forces developers to write cleaner, more modular code. It ensures that each function behaves as expected in isolation.
- **Refactoring with Confidence**: With a robust suite of unit tests in place, you can refactor your code without the fear of breaking existing functionality.
- **Documentation**: Unit tests serve as live documentation for how your code is intended to work. They demonstrate the expected behavior of methods and classes.

Writing Unit Tests in C# with xUnit

Setting Up the Testing Environment

In this section, we'll walk you through the process of setting up your environment for unit testing using **xUnit**.

1. **Install xUnit**:
   - Open your project in **Visual Studio**.
   - Right-click on your solution and select **Manage NuGet Packages for Solution**.
   - Search for **xUnit** and install it.
2. **Create a Test Project**:
   - In Visual Studio, create a new **xUnit Test Project**:
     - Go to **File > New > Project**.
     - Choose **xUnit Test Project** and give it a name, such as `ECommerceApp.Tests`.
     - This project will contain all your test classes.
3. **Set Up the Test Framework**:

     o   Your test project should have a reference to the main project where the code you want to test resides. To add the reference:
- Right-click on the **Dependencies** folder in the test project.
- Click **Add Reference** and select your main project (e.g., `ECommerceApp`).

The Anatomy of a Unit Test

A unit test typically consists of three main parts:

1. **Arrange:** Set up the necessary objects and prepare the environment.
2. **Act:** Invoke the method or functionality you're testing.
3. **Assert:** Verify that the result is what you expected.

A typical unit test looks like this:

```csharp
[Fact]
public void TestTaxCalculation()
{
    // Arrange
    var order = new Order { Amount = 100.0 };
    var taxCalculator = new TaxCalculator();

    // Act
    var result = taxCalculator.CalculateTax(order);

    // Assert
    Assert.Equal(10.0, result);
}
```

In this example:

- **Arrange**: We create an `Order` object with a specified amount and a `TaxCalculator` object.
- **Act**: We call the `CalculateTax` method to get the tax for the order.
- **Assert**: We check that the calculated tax is equal to the expected value (in this case, `10.0`).

Hands-On Project: Writing Unit Tests for a Tax Calculation Function

Problem Statement

In an e-commerce application, you need to calculate the tax for an order. The tax rate is **10%** of the order's total amount. Your task is to write a function that calculates the tax for an order and then write unit tests for that function.

Step 1: Create the Function to Calculate Tax

First, let's create a simple class called `TaxCalculator` that has a method called `CalculateTax`. This function will take an `Order` object as input and return the calculated tax.

Create a class called `TaxCalculator.cs`:

```csharp
namespace ECommerceApp
{
    public class TaxCalculator
    {
        public double CalculateTax(Order order)
        {
            if (order == null)
```

```
            throw new
ArgumentNullException(nameof(order));

            return order.Amount * 0.10;  // Tax rate
is 10%
        }
    }

    public class Order
    {
        public double Amount { get; set; }
    }
}
```

Step 2: Write Unit Tests for the Tax Calculation

Next, let's write unit tests for the `CalculateTax` method. Create a test class called `TaxCalculatorTests.cs` in the test project:

csharp

```
using Xunit;
using ECommerceApp;

namespace ECommerceApp.Tests
{
    public class TaxCalculatorTests
    {
        [Fact]
        public void
CalculateTax_WithValidAmount_ReturnsCorrectTax()
        {
            // Arrange
            var order = new Order { Amount = 100.0 };
            var taxCalculator = new TaxCalculator();

            // Act
            var result =
taxCalculator.CalculateTax(order);

            // Assert
            Assert.Equal(10.0, result);
        }
```

```csharp
[Fact]
public void
CalculateTax_WithZeroAmount_ReturnsZeroTax()
    {
        // Arrange
        var order = new Order { Amount = 0.0 };
        var taxCalculator = new TaxCalculator();

        // Act
        var result =
taxCalculator.CalculateTax(order);

        // Assert
        Assert.Equal(0.0, result);
    }

[Fact]
public void
CalculateTax_WithNegativeAmount_ThrowsArgumentExcepti
on()
    {
        // Arrange
        var order = new Order { Amount = -100.0
};
        var taxCalculator = new TaxCalculator();

        // Act & Assert
        Assert.Throws<ArgumentException>(() =>
taxCalculator.CalculateTax(order));
    }

[Fact]
public void
CalculateTax_WithNullOrder_ThrowsArgumentNullExceptio
n()
    {
        // Arrange
        TaxCalculator taxCalculator = new
TaxCalculator();

        // Act & Assert
        Assert.Throws<ArgumentNullException>(()
=> taxCalculator.CalculateTax(null));
```

```
            }
        }
    }
```

Explanation of the Unit Tests:

- **Test 1: CalculateTax_WithValidAmount_ReturnsCorrectTax**: This test ensures that when an order with a valid amount is passed, the calculated tax is correct.
- **Test 2: CalculateTax_WithZeroAmount_ReturnsZeroTax**: This test checks that when the order amount is zero, the tax calculated is also zero.
- **Test 3: CalculateTax_WithNegativeAmount_ThrowsArgumentException**: This test ensures that the method throws an exception when the order amount is negative.
- **Test 4: CalculateTax_WithNullOrder_ThrowsArgumentNullException**: This test ensures that the method throws an exception when a `null` order is passed to the method.

Step 3: Run the Unit Tests

Now that we've written our unit tests, let's run them:

1. Open the **Test Explorer** in Visual Studio (`Test > Windows > Test Explorer`).
2. Click **Run All** to run all tests.
3. Verify that all tests pass successfully.

Real-World Application: Unit Testing in Business-Critical Applications

Why Unit Testing is Crucial for Business-Critical Applications

In real-world applications, especially business-critical systems like **e-commerce platforms**, **inventory management systems**, or **financial applications**, ensuring that your code behaves as expected is vital. Errors in these applications could lead to lost revenue, damaged customer trust, or even legal consequences.

Unit tests allow developers to:

- **Identify issues early**: Catch errors before they make it to production.
- **Ensure consistency**: Confirm that features behave as expected across different versions of the software.

- **Improve maintainability**: Refactor code confidently, knowing that tests will catch any issues that arise from changes.

Example: E-Commerce Application

In an **e-commerce** application, unit tests could be used to ensure the reliability of various critical functions, such as:

- **Price calculation**: Ensuring that the final price after applying discounts and taxes is correct.
- **Payment processing**: Verifying that payments are correctly handled and transactions are accurately recorded.
- **Inventory management**: Ensuring that stock levels are accurately updated after purchases or returns.

By writing comprehensive unit tests for these key business functions, you can help ensure the smooth operation of the application and provide confidence that it will perform correctly in production.

Conclusion

In this chapter, we introduced you to the concept of **unit testing** in C#, why it's an essential practice in software development, and how it contributes to building reliable, high-quality applications. You wrote unit tests for a **tax calculation function** in an e-commerce application and learned how to test for valid input, edge cases, and exceptions.

As you develop more complex systems, the ability to write effective unit tests will be invaluable in ensuring that your codebase remains stable and reliable, especially in business-critical applications. In the next chapter, we'll explore **dependency injection** in C#, which is an essential pattern for building scalable and testable applications.

Happy coding, and keep writing those tests!

Chapter 7: Exploring Unity Game Development with C#

Introduction to Unity Game Development with C#

Welcome to an exciting chapter where we will dive into **Unity game development with C#**! Unity is one of the most popular game engines used by both amateur and professional developers to create 2D and 3D games. Its versatility and ease of use make it an excellent platform for developing games, simulations, and interactive experiences for a wide range of industries, from entertainment to education.

In this chapter, we will cover essential Unity-specific C# skills, including creating and manipulating **game objects**, handling **user input**, and understanding the core components of **Unity's physics engine**. By the end of the chapter, you will have developed a simple **2D platformer or puzzle game** complete with interactive elements.

Unity provides a robust framework for creating dynamic, engaging experiences, and C# is the primary language used for scripting gameplay logic, controlling objects, and interacting with the Unity environment. Whether you're building your first game or aiming to sharpen your skills, this chapter will guide you through the process of creating your own interactive game in Unity.

What You'll Need

Before we dive into the game development process, let's make sure you have everything set up and ready to go.

Software Requirements:

1. **Unity Hub and Unity Editor:**
   - Download and install **Unity Hub** from the official Unity website. Unity Hub is the launcher that helps you manage different versions of Unity.
   - Install the latest **Unity Editor** through Unity Hub. Make sure you include support for **2D Game Development** during installation.
2. **Visual Studio:**
   - Visual Studio is the primary IDE used for Unity development. It provides features like IntelliSense, debugging tools, and syntax highlighting for C#.
   - **Download:** Visual Studio Community Edition, which integrates seamlessly with Unity, can be downloaded from Visual Studio's website.
3. **Unity Assets:**
   - For our hands-on project, we will be using **free assets** available from the Unity Asset Store or creating simple assets ourselves (e.g., shapes for 2D characters and objects). These assets can be downloaded from the Asset Store within Unity.

Hardware Requirements:

- **A computer** with at least **4GB of RAM** (8GB or more is recommended for smoother performance). Unity can be demanding, so the better your system, the more efficient the development process will be.

Prerequisites:

- **Basic C# Knowledge:** You should have a solid understanding of C# syntax and object-oriented programming (OOP). If you're new to C#, be sure to go through the earlier chapters on C# basics before proceeding with Unity.
- **Basic Game Development Concepts**: A general understanding of game development concepts (e.g., 2D game mechanics, game loops, and basic physics) will be beneficial but is not required.

Chapter Overview

In this chapter, we will:

1. **Understand the Unity Environment**: Learn how to navigate the Unity Editor and set up a new project.
2. **Create and Manipulate Game Objects**: Learn how to create game objects and interact with them using C# scripts.
3. **Handle User Input**: Implement player controls for movement and interaction.

4. **Understand Unity's Physics Engine**: Learn how Unity's physics engine works and how to apply forces and collisions.
5. **Hands-On Project**: Build a simple **2D platformer or puzzle game** with interactive elements.

---

1. Understanding the Unity Environment

Getting Started with Unity

When you first open Unity, you'll be greeted by the **Unity Hub**, which helps you manage projects, versions of Unity, and various settings. From here, you can create a new project or open an existing one.

1. **Create a New Project**:
   o Launch Unity Hub.
   o Click on the "New" button to create a new project.
   o Select **2D** as the project template (since we will be building a 2D game in this chapter).
   o Name your project (e.g., **MyFirstPlatformer**) and choose a location to save it.
   o Click **Create**.
2. **Unity Editor Layout**:
   o The Unity Editor is divided into several panels, the most important of which are:
      ▪ **Scene View**: The main area where you build and edit your game.
      ▪ **Game View**: Shows how your game will appear to the player.
      ▪ **Hierarchy**: Lists all the game objects in your scene.

- **Inspector**: Allows you to modify the properties of selected game objects.
- **Project**: Shows all the files and assets in your project, such as textures, scripts, and scenes.
- **Console**: Displays logs, errors, and debug information.

---

2. Creating and Manipulating Game Objects

In Unity, everything you see in your game, such as characters, platforms, and obstacles, is a **game object**. These objects can be 2D sprites, 3D models, lights, cameras, and more. In this section, we'll create some basic game objects for our 2D platformer.

Creating a Game Object (Player)

1. **Add a Player Object**:
   o Right-click in the **Hierarchy** panel and choose **2D Object > Sprite**. This creates a new sprite in the scene.
   o Rename the sprite to `Player` by right-clicking on the object in the **Hierarchy** and selecting **Rename**.
   o In the **Inspector**, under the **Sprite Renderer** component, click the small circle next to **Sprite** and choose a sprite for the player (you can use a default square sprite or an image from the Unity Asset Store).
2. **Add Movement to the Player**:

- o Create a C# script to control the player's movement. Right-click in the **Project** panel, go to **Create > C# Script,** and name it `PlayerController`.
- o Double-click the script to open it in Visual Studio.
- o Replace the default code with the following:

```csharp
using UnityEngine;

public class PlayerController : MonoBehaviour
{
    public float moveSpeed = 5f;

    private void Update()
    {
        // Get horizontal input
        float moveInput =
Input.GetAxis("Horizontal");

        // Move the player
        transform.Translate(Vector2.right * moveInput
* moveSpeed * Time.deltaTime);
    }
}
```

- • **Explanation:**
  - o **Input.GetAxis("Horizontal"):** This gets the player's input from the keyboard (arrow keys or "A" and "D" keys by default).
  - o **transform.Translate:** Moves the player's position based on the input.
- • **Attach the Script:** Drag and drop the `PlayerController` script onto the `Player` object in the **Hierarchy** panel.

3. Handling User Input

In Unity, user input is typically handled via the **Input class**. The player can interact with the game through the keyboard, mouse, or touch input.

Implementing Jumping Mechanism

Let's now implement a basic **jumping mechanic** using the **space bar**. To do this, we'll need to handle physics and gravity.

1. **Add a Rigidbody2D Component:**
   - Select the `Player` object in the **Hierarchy**.
   - In the **Inspector**, click **Add Component** and search for **Rigidbody2D**.
   - The Rigidbody2D component is used to handle the physics of the player, such as gravity and collisions.
2. **Update the PlayerController Script for Jumping:**
   - Modify the `PlayerController` script to include jumping:

```csharp
using UnityEngine;

public class PlayerController : MonoBehaviour
{
    public float moveSpeed = 5f;
    public float jumpForce = 10f;

    private Rigidbody2D rb;

    private void Start()
    {
        rb = GetComponent<Rigidbody2D>();
    }
```

```
private void Update()
{
    // Get horizontal input
    float moveInput =
Input.GetAxis("Horizontal");
    transform.Translate(Vector2.right * moveInput
* moveSpeed * Time.deltaTime);

    // Jumping logic
    if (Input.GetKeyDown(KeyCode.Space))
    {
        rb.velocity = new Vector2(rb.velocity.x,
jumpForce);
    }
  }
}
```

- **Explanation**:
    - **Rigidbody2D**: We use this component to apply physics-based movement, including jumping.
    - **Input.GetKeyDown(KeyCode.Space)**: Detects when the player presses the space bar.
    - **rb.velocity**: Sets the velocity of the player, applying the jump force along the y-axis.

4. Understanding Unity's Physics Engine

Unity's physics engine is built on two components: **Rigidbody2D** and **Collider2D**. These components allow objects to interact with each other through collisions, forces, and gravity. In this section, we'll explore how to use Unity's physics engine to add realistic movement and interactions.

Adding Platforms and Collisions

To allow the player to interact with the environment, we need to add **colliders** to both the player and the platforms.

1. **Add a Platform**:
   - Right-click in the **Hierarchy** and create a **2D Object > Sprite** to represent a platform.
   - Resize the sprite to a larger size and name it `Platform`.
   - Add a **BoxCollider2D** component to the platform (this allows it to interact with other objects physically).
2. **Ensure the Player Lands on the Platform**:
   - Ensure the **Player** object has a **BoxCollider2D** component attached to it.
   - Make sure that the **Player** object has a **Rigidbody2D** component for physics interactions.

Now, when the player jumps, they will land on the platform, and the physics engine will handle the interaction.

---

5. Hands-On Project: Simple 2D Platformer

Now, let's combine everything we've learned so far to build a simple 2D platformer with a player character that can move and jump.

Step 1: Create a Simple Level

1. **Create a Ground Platform**: Use a **2D Sprite** to create a ground platform for the player to walk on.
2. **Add Obstacles**: Add some obstacles using simple shapes (e.g., a rectangular block with a **BoxCollider2D**).
3. **Player Movement**: Make sure the player can move horizontally and jump to avoid obstacles.

Step 2: Implement a Collectible Item

1. **Create a Coin Object**: Add a coin (or any item) to the scene.
2. **Add Interactivity**: When the player collides with the coin, increase their score.

Here's a script to handle the coin collection:

```csharp
using UnityEngine;

public class Coin : MonoBehaviour
{
    public int scoreValue = 1;

    private void OnTriggerEnter2D(Collider2D other)
    {
        if (other.CompareTag("Player"))
        {
            // Increase the score

ScoreManager.Instance.AddScore(scoreValue);

            // Destroy the coin
            Destroy(gameObject);
        }
    }
}
```

```
}
```

Explanation:

- The coin is destroyed when the player touches it, and the score is updated.

Step 3: Add Score Management

Create a **ScoreManager** script to track and display the score.

csharp

```csharp
using UnityEngine;
using UnityEngine.UI;

public class ScoreManager : MonoBehaviour
{
    public static ScoreManager Instance;
    public Text scoreText;
    private int score;

    private void Awake()
    {
        if (Instance == null)
        {
            Instance = this;
        }
    }

    public void AddScore(int value)
    {
        score += value;
        scoreText.text = "Score: " + score;
    }
}
```

6. Real-World Application: Unity in Business and Education

Unity is not just for entertainment and gaming. It is also widely used in **education, training simulations**, and **interactive media**.

- **Education**: Unity is used to create interactive learning experiences and educational simulations that can be used in classrooms or for online courses.
- **Healthcare**: Virtual simulations and training applications are built using Unity to simulate medical procedures or teach students about anatomy.
- **Manufacturing and Engineering**: Unity is used in simulation software to visualize complex data or products.

Conclusion

In this chapter, we explored the core concepts of **Unity game development with C#**, including creating game objects, handling user input, and understanding Unity's physics engine. We also completed a hands-on project to build a simple **2D platformer** where the player can move, jump, and collect items.

Unity's versatility allows you to create a wide variety of interactive applications, whether you're building games for entertainment or educational experiences for the classroom. By mastering these foundational skills, you'll be well-equipped to develop engaging and interactive applications for various industries.

In the next chapter, we will dive into **advanced game mechanics**, such as AI, pathfinding, and animations, to make your games even more dynamic and exciting. Keep practicing, and happy developing!

Chapter 8: Multithreading in C#

Introduction to Multithreading in C#

In the world of modern software development, performance is often a key consideration, especially for applications that need to handle multiple tasks at the same time. This is where **multithreading** comes in. Multithreading allows a program to run multiple operations concurrently, making it much more efficient and responsive, especially when it comes to resource-intensive tasks like downloading files, processing large datasets, or rendering complex graphics.

In this chapter, we will explore the core concepts of **multithreading** in **C#**, how it works, and when to use it for performance optimization. We'll dive into how to manage threads, share data between them, and tackle common challenges such as race conditions and deadlocks. Finally, we'll walk through a hands-on project where we'll build a **multithreaded downloader** that fetches files concurrently from the internet.

By the end of this chapter, you'll have a solid understanding of multithreading in C#, and you'll be able to apply these techniques to your own applications to improve their performance.

What You'll Need

Before we dive into the concepts of multithreading, let's make sure you're ready to follow along with the hands-on project.

Software Requirements:

1. **Visual Studio**:
   - The **IDE** of choice for C# development is **Visual Studio**. It includes powerful tools for debugging, writing code, and managing project dependencies.
   - **Download**: Visual Studio Community Edition can be downloaded from Visual Studio's website.
2. **.NET SDK**:
   - **.NET Core SDK** is required for building C# applications. If you haven't already installed it, download it from Microsoft's .NET download page.
3. **Web Browser**:
   - We'll be downloading files from the internet in our hands-on project, so any modern web browser will do.

Hardware Requirements:

- A **computer** with at least **4GB of RAM** is recommended. More memory and a powerful processor will be beneficial for handling intensive tasks in multithreading projects.

Prerequisites:

- **Basic C# Knowledge**: You should be familiar with basic C# syntax, object-oriented programming, and working with classes and methods.
- **Basic Understanding of Threads**: A basic knowledge of how threads work and the concept of parallelism will help, but we'll cover the essentials in this chapter.

Chapter Overview

In this chapter, we will:

1. **Understand Multithreading**: Learn the fundamental concepts behind multithreading, how threads work, and why you need them.
2. **Create and Manage Threads**: Explore how to create and manage threads in C# and understand the lifecycle of a thread.
3. **Handle Thread Safety**: Learn how to handle data sharing between threads and prevent common issues like **race conditions**.
4. **Hands-On Project**: Build a **multithreaded downloader** to fetch files concurrently from the internet.
5. **Real-World Application**: Apply multithreading to optimize performance in real-world scenarios, such as video editing software.

1. Understanding Multithreading in C#

What Is a Thread?

A **thread** is the smallest unit of execution in a program. Every program has at least one thread: the main thread, which runs the program's instructions. However, by using **multithreading**, you can run multiple threads concurrently, which allows your program to handle multiple tasks simultaneously.

Why Use Multithreading?

Multithreading is especially useful for tasks that can run independently or in parallel, such as:

- **Downloading multiple files** at once.
- **Processing data** in parallel (e.g., processing large files or images).
- **Handling user input** while performing background tasks (e.g., downloading, calculations).

Basic Concepts of Multithreading

- **Main Thread**: This is the thread that starts when you run your program. It's responsible for starting and managing other threads.
- **Worker Threads**: These are threads that perform tasks in the background, such as downloading files, processing data, or updating UI elements.

How Multithreading Works in C#

In C#, the `System.Threading` namespace provides the necessary tools to create and manage threads.

Here's an example of creating a basic thread in C#:

```csharp
using System;
using System.Threading;

class Program
{
    static void Main()
    {
        Thread myThread = new Thread(DoWork);
        myThread.Start();   // Start the thread

        Console.WriteLine("Main thread is running");
        myThread.Join();   // Wait for the thread to
finish
    }

    static void DoWork()
    {
        Console.WriteLine("Worker thread is
running");
    }
}
```

Explanation:

- **Thread myThread = new Thread(DoWork);:** Creates a new thread that will execute the `DoWork` method.
- **myThread.Start();:** Starts the new thread.
- **myThread.Join();:** Waits for the worker thread to complete before the main thread continues.

This example demonstrates how to create a basic thread that performs a task independently of the main thread.

2. Creating and Managing Threads

Creating Threads in C#

To create a thread in C#, you use the `Thread` class from the `System.Threading` namespace. When creating a thread, you can pass a method that the thread will execute. This method should contain the logic you want to execute in parallel.

Example: Creating a Thread to Print Numbers
csharp

```csharp
using System;
using System.Threading;

class Program
{
    static void Main()
    {
        Thread t1 = new Thread(PrintNumbers);
        t1.Start();

        Thread t2 = new Thread(PrintNumbers);
        t2.Start();
    }

    static void PrintNumbers()
    {
        for (int i = 1; i <= 5; i++)
        {
            Console.WriteLine(i);
            Thread.Sleep(1000);  // Simulate some
work by pausing the thread for 1 second
        }
    }
}
```

Explanation:

- We create two threads, `t1` and `t2`, both of which execute the `PrintNumbers` method.
- The `Thread.Sleep(1000)` method pauses the thread for 1 second to simulate some work (e.g., downloading a file).

Managing Thread Life Cycle

- **Start()**: Starts the execution of a thread.
- **Join()**: Waits for the thread to complete its execution.
- **Abort()**: Terminates the thread prematurely (not recommended for general use).
- **Sleep()**: Pauses the thread for a specified amount of time.

Thread Pooling

In most cases, creating a new thread for each task may not be efficient, especially when handling a large number of threads. Instead, you can use **thread pooling** via the `ThreadPool` class, which reuses threads from a pool of available threads.

```csharp
using System;
using System.Threading;

class Program
{
    static void Main()
    {
        // Queue work item to thread pool
        ThreadPool.QueueUserWorkItem(DoWork);
        Console.WriteLine("Main thread is continuing...");
    }

    static void DoWork(object state)
```

```
    {
        Console.WriteLine("Worker thread is doing
work");
    }
}
```

Explanation:

- The `ThreadPool.QueueUserWorkItem()` method queues a method for execution by a thread pool thread.

---

3. Handling Thread Safety

When multiple threads are accessing shared data, it's essential to ensure that the data is manipulated safely. If multiple threads access the same data simultaneously, it can lead to **race conditions**, where the final outcome depends on the order in which threads execute.

Race Conditions and Synchronization

A **race condition** occurs when two threads attempt to modify shared data at the same time. To prevent this, we can use **synchronization** mechanisms such as **locks**.

Example: Using Locks to Ensure Thread Safety
csharp

```
using System;
using System.Threading;

class Program
{
    static int counter = 0;
    static object lockObj = new object();   // Lock
object
```

```
static void Main()
{
    Thread t1 = new Thread(IncrementCounter);
    Thread t2 = new Thread(IncrementCounter);

    t1.Start();
    t2.Start();

    t1.Join();
    t2.Join();

    Console.WriteLine("Counter: " + counter);
}

static void IncrementCounter()
{
    for (int i = 0; i < 1000; i++)
    {
        lock (lockObj)  // Ensure only one thread
accesses the counter at a time
        {
            counter++;
        }
    }
}
}
```

Explanation:

- The `lock (lockObj)` statement ensures that only one thread can execute the code inside the lock at a time, preventing race conditions.

Other Synchronization Mechanisms

- **Mutex:** A synchronization primitive that is used to manage access to resources across different threads or processes.

- **Semaphore**: A signaling mechanism that controls access to a resource pool.
- **Monitor**: Provides a mechanism for managing synchronization in multithreaded environments.

4. Hands-On Project: Multithreaded File Downloader

In this hands-on project, we'll build a **multithreaded downloader** that fetches files from the internet concurrently. This is an excellent example of how to use multithreading to optimize performance when dealing with multiple I/O-bound tasks like downloading files.

Step 1: Create a New Console Application

Start by creating a new **Console Application** in Visual Studio.

Step 2: Add the Download Logic

1. Create a class called `FileDownloader.cs`:

csharp

```
using System;
using System.Net;
using System.Threading;

class FileDownloader
{
    public void DownloadFile(string url, string
destination)
    {
        using (WebClient client = new WebClient())
        {
            client.DownloadFile(url, destination);
            Console.WriteLine($"Downloaded file from
{url} to {destination}");
        }
    }
}
```

2. In the `Main` method, start multiple threads to download files concurrently:

csharp

```
class Program
{
    static void Main()
    {
        FileDownloader downloader = new
FileDownloader();

        string[] urls = new string[]
```

```
        {
            "https://example.com/file1.zip",
            "https://example.com/file2.zip",
            "https://example.com/file3.zip"
        };

        string[] destinations = new string[]
        {
            "file1.zip",
            "file2.zip",
            "file3.zip"
        };

        // Start downloading files concurrently using
threads
        for (int i = 0; i < urls.Length; i++)
        {
            int index = i;  // Capture the index for
closure
            Thread t = new Thread(() =>
downloader.DownloadFile(urls[index],
destinations[index]));
            t.Start();
        }

        Console.WriteLine("All downloads are
started.");
    }
}
```

Explanation:

- The DownloadFile method downloads a file from a given URL and saves it to the destination.
- We use a loop to start a new thread for each file download, allowing them to run concurrently.

Step 3: Run the Application

When you run this application, it will download the files concurrently, optimizing the total download time. You'll see multiple downloads happening at once, which would be much slower if done sequentially.

5. Real-World Application: Optimizing Performance

In real-world applications, multithreading can be a game-changer for performance, particularly when dealing with tasks like video processing, data analysis, and large-scale web scraping.

For example, in **video editing software**, you might need to apply filters to frames, render previews, or handle multiple video streams. Multithreading can allow the software to perform these tasks concurrently, making it faster and more responsive.

In **manufacturing** or **logistics applications**, multithreading can be used to process large amounts of data from sensors or devices, perform simulations, and run background calculations.

Conclusion

In this chapter, we learned the fundamentals of **multithreading in C#** and explored how to use threads to optimize performance in your applications. You learned how to create threads, manage their lifecycle, and handle thread safety issues like race conditions.

By completing the **multithreaded downloader** project, you've gained hands-on experience with managing multiple threads for concurrent tasks. This is just the beginning! Multithreading is an essential tool for optimizing performance in many types of applications, especially those that need to handle multiple tasks at once.

In the next chapter, we will explore more advanced **concurrent programming** techniques, such as **asynchronous programming** with `async` and `await`, and how these can be combined with multithreading for even more powerful performance optimization. Keep experimenting, and happy coding!

Chapter 9: Working with APIs and Web Services

Introduction to APIs and Web Services

In the modern world of software development, **APIs** (Application Programming Interfaces) are essential tools that allow different software systems to communicate and share data. Whether you're developing a mobile app, a website, or even an enterprise system, chances are you will need to interact with external APIs and web services to enrich your application.

In this chapter, we will explore how to **consume RESTful APIs** using **HttpClient** in **C#**. We will build a practical **weather app** that pulls data from a weather API and displays it to the user. This hands-on approach will help you understand how to interact with APIs and use the data in your applications. Additionally, we will look at real-world applications of API integration, such as connecting with **payment gateways** or **social media platforms**.

By the end of this chapter, you will have a solid understanding of how to consume and interact with APIs and how to make HTTP requests in C#. You will also learn how to handle data and errors effectively when working with APIs.

What You'll Need

Before we dive into building the weather app, let's ensure you have everything set up to follow along with this chapter.

Software Requirements:

1. **Visual Studio**:
   - **Visual Studio** is the primary Integrated Development Environment (IDE) for C# development. It provides a rich development experience for writing, debugging, and testing C# applications.
   - **Download**: You can download **Visual Studio Community Edition** from Visual Studio's website.
2. **.NET SDK**:
   - The **.NET SDK** is required to run and develop C# applications. Make sure you have the SDK installed on your machine.
   - You can download it from Microsoft's .NET download page.
3. **Weather API**:
   - For our hands-on project, we will use a **free weather API**. A good choice for this is the **OpenWeatherMap API**.
   - Go to OpenWeatherMap and sign up for a free account. After signing up, you will receive an API key, which you will use to make requests.
4. **Postman** (optional):
   - **Postman** is a great tool for testing API requests before integrating them into your application. You can use Postman to make requests to the

weather API and view the responses in a user-friendly interface.

Hardware Requirements:

- A **computer** with at least **4GB of RAM** is recommended. A more powerful computer with more memory will provide a smoother experience, especially when dealing with multiple applications running simultaneously.

Prerequisites:

- **Basic C# Knowledge**: You should be comfortable with basic C# syntax, object-oriented programming (OOP), and concepts like classes, methods, and properties.
- **Understanding of HTTP Requests**: Having a basic understanding of how the web works and the concept of HTTP requests (GET, POST, etc.) will be helpful, but we'll explain everything as we go along.
- **Basic JSON Handling**: Familiarity with JSON (JavaScript Object Notation), which is a common format used by APIs to exchange data, is useful but not required. We'll cover how to work with JSON data in this chapter.

Chapter Overview

In this chapter, we will cover:

1. **What an API is**: We'll introduce the concept of APIs, how they work, and how to interact with them.

2. **Making HTTP Requests in C#**: Learn how to use the `HttpClient` class to make HTTP requests and retrieve data from APIs.
3. **Working with JSON**: Learn how to parse and handle JSON data received from an API.
4. **Hands-On Project**: We will build a simple **weather app** that interacts with a weather API and displays the weather data to the user.
5. **Real-World Applications**: We will look at real-world examples of how APIs are used in various industries, such as integrating **payment gateways** and **social media**.

1. What is an API?

An **API** (Application Programming Interface) is a set of rules that allows one software program to communicate with another. It provides a way for applications to interact with each other, share data, and perform actions. APIs allow developers to access the functionality of other applications or services without needing to understand the underlying code.

There are different types of APIs, but in this chapter, we will focus on **RESTful APIs**, which are the most common. REST (Representational State Transfer) is an architectural style for designing networked applications. RESTful APIs use HTTP methods such as GET, POST, PUT, and DELETE to interact with resources (data).

Common HTTP Methods:

- **GET**: Retrieve data from a server (e.g., fetching weather data).
- **POST**: Send data to a server (e.g., submitting a form or creating a new record).
- **PUT**: Update existing data on the server (e.g., updating a user profile).
- **DELETE**: Delete data from the server.

How APIs Are Used in the Real World:

- **Payment Gateways**: APIs allow you to integrate payment processing into your applications (e.g., PayPal, Stripe).
- **Social Media**: APIs allow you to interact with social media platforms like Facebook, Twitter, and Instagram (e.g., posting updates, fetching user data).
- **Weather Services**: APIs provide real-time data from weather services (e.g., OpenWeatherMap API).
- **Geolocation**: APIs are used to retrieve maps, location data, and geospatial services (e.g., Google Maps API).

2. Making HTTP Requests in C#

HttpClient in C#

To interact with APIs in C#, we typically use the `HttpClient` class. This class provides methods to send HTTP requests and receive responses. It is part of the `System.Net.Http` namespace.

Creating an HttpClient Instance:

Before you can use `HttpClient`, you need to create an instance of it. Here's a basic example of how to make a **GET request** to an API:

csharp

```
using System;
using System.Net.Http;
using System.Threading.Tasks;

class Program
{
    static async Task Main(string[] args)
    {
        using (HttpClient client = new HttpClient())
        {
            // Set the base address for the API
            client.BaseAddress = new
Uri("https://api.openweathermap.org/data/2.5/");

            // Make a GET request to the weather API
(using a sample endpoint)
            HttpResponseMessage response = await
client.GetAsync("weather?q=London&appid=your_api_key"
);

            // Ensure the response is successful
            response.EnsureSuccessStatusCode();

            // Read and output the response content
            string content = await
response.Content.ReadAsStringAsync();
            Console.WriteLine(content);
        }
    }
}
```

Explanation:

- **HttpClient client = new HttpClient()**: Creates an instance of `HttpClient` to send requests.
- **client.GetAsync**: Sends an asynchronous GET request to the specified API endpoint.
- **response.EnsureSuccessStatusCode()**: Throws an exception if the response indicates failure (e.g., 404 or 500).
- **response.Content.ReadAsStringAsync()**: Reads the response body as a string.

Error Handling in HttpClient

When working with APIs, it's important to handle errors such as timeouts, invalid requests, or server errors. Here's an example that includes error handling:

csharp

```
try
{
    HttpResponseMessage response = await
client.GetAsync("weather?q=London&appid=your_api_key"
);

    if (response.IsSuccessStatusCode)
    {
        string data = await
response.Content.ReadAsStringAsync();
        Console.WriteLine(data);
    }
    else
    {
        Console.WriteLine("Error: " +
response.StatusCode);
    }
}
catch (HttpRequestException e)
{
    Console.WriteLine("Request error: " + e.Message);
```

```
}
```

---

3. Working with JSON

Most APIs return data in **JSON** (JavaScript Object Notation) format. In C#, we can use the `Newtonsoft.Json` library (also known as **Json.NET**) to parse and work with JSON data.

Install Newtonsoft.Json:

To get started with **Newtonsoft.Json,** install the package via NuGet:

```bash
Install-Package Newtonsoft.Json
```

Parsing JSON Data:

Here's how to parse JSON data returned from an API. Let's assume the weather API returns data like this:

```json
{
    "weather": [
        {
            "description": "clear sky"
        }
    ],
    "main": {
        "temp": 22.5
    }
}
```

We can create C# classes to represent the data:

```csharp
```

```
public class Weather
{
    public List<WeatherDescription> weather { get;
set; }
    public Main main { get; set; }
}

public class WeatherDescription
{
    public string description { get; set; }
}

public class Main
{
    public double temp { get; set; }
}
```

Now, you can parse the JSON response:

csharp

```
using Newtonsoft.Json;

string jsonResponse = await
response.Content.ReadAsStringAsync();
Weather weatherData =
JsonConvert.DeserializeObject<Weather>(jsonResponse);

Console.WriteLine("Weather Description: " +
weatherData.weather[0].description);
Console.WriteLine("Temperature: " +
weatherData.main.temp + "°C");
```

Explanation:

- **JsonConvert.DeserializeObject<Weather>**:
  Deserializes the JSON string into a C# object of type
  `Weather`.
- **weatherData.weather[0].description**: Accesses the
  weather description.

- **weatherData.main.temp**: Accesses the temperature.

---

4. Hands-On Project: Building a Weather App

Now that we understand how to make API requests and work with JSON, let's put it all together and build a simple **weather app**.

Step 1: Create a New Console Application

1. Open Visual Studio and create a new **Console Application** project.
2. Name the project WeatherApp.

Step 2: Install Dependencies

1. Install Newtonsoft.Json via NuGet to handle JSON parsing.
2. Install System.Net.Http to handle HTTP requests.

Step 3: Implement the Weather Fetching Logic

In the Program.cs file, implement the logic to fetch weather data using the OpenWeatherMap API:

csharp

```
using System;
using System.Net.Http;
using System.Threading.Tasks;
using Newtonsoft.Json;

class Program
{
    static async Task Main(string[] args)
```

```csharp
        {
            Console.Write("Enter city name: ");
            string city = Console.ReadLine();

            string apiKey = "your_api_key";   // Replace
with your actual API key
            string url =
$"https://api.openweathermap.org/data/2.5/weather?q={
city}&appid={apiKey}&units=metric";

            using (HttpClient client = new HttpClient())
            {
                try
                {
                    HttpResponseMessage response = await
client.GetAsync(url);
                    response.EnsureSuccessStatusCode();

                    string content = await
response.Content.ReadAsStringAsync();
                    Weather weather =
JsonConvert.DeserializeObject<Weather>(content);

                    Console.WriteLine($"Weather in
{city}: {weather.weather[0].description}");
                    Console.WriteLine($"Temperature:
{weather.main.temp}°C");
                }
                catch (HttpRequestException e)
                {
                    Console.WriteLine("Error: " +
e.Message);
                }
            }
        }
}

public class Weather
{
    public List<WeatherDescription> weather { get;
set; }
    public Main main { get; set; }
}
```

```
public class WeatherDescription
{
    public string description { get; set; }
}

public class Main
{
    public double temp { get; set; }
}
```

Explanation:

- The program asks for the user's input (city name) and fetches the weather data from the OpenWeatherMap API.
- The JSON response is deserialized into the `Weather` class, and the weather information is displayed to the user.

Step 4: Run the Application

1. Enter the name of a city (e.g., "London" or "New York").
2. The app will display the weather description and temperature for the entered city.

---

5. Real-World Application: API Integration

APIs are not limited to weather data. In the real world, APIs are used for various purposes such as:

- **Payment Gateways**: Integrating services like **Stripe**, **PayPal**, or **Square** for processing payments.

- **Social Media APIs**: Posting updates, reading user data, and interacting with services like **Facebook, Twitter**, or **Instagram**.
- **Shipping and Logistics**: Using APIs from carriers like **FedEx, UPS**, or **DHL** for real-time tracking.
- **News and Content**: Fetching content from news agencies, blogs, or aggregators.

Example: Integrating a Payment API

For example, if you were integrating **Stripe** for payments, the API would allow you to securely process credit card payments within your application. This would involve sending payment information to the Stripe API and receiving a confirmation or failure response.

Conclusion

In this chapter, we've covered the essentials of working with **APIs** in C#, from making HTTP requests to handling JSON responses. We built a simple **weather app** that pulls real-time weather data from an API and displays it to the user. This project helped demonstrate the power of APIs in extending the functionality of your applications.

Real-world applications of API integration are limitless, from payment processing to social media management and beyond. As you continue building your software, you'll frequently encounter scenarios where interacting with external services is essential.

Chapter 10: Creating Cross-Platform Mobile Apps with Xamarin

Introduction to Xamarin and Cross-Platform Mobile Development

In the fast-evolving world of mobile development, building apps that work on both **Android** and **iOS** with a single codebase is a dream for many developers. Historically, developers had to write separate code for each platform, which resulted in increased development time, cost, and complexity. However, **Xamarin**, a powerful cross-platform mobile app development framework, has changed the game.

In this chapter, we will explore Xamarin and its capabilities to build cross-platform mobile apps using **C#**. Xamarin allows you to write your app once, and then run it on both Android and iOS with minimal changes. Whether you're building a simple to-do list app or a complex enterprise solution, Xamarin helps you save time and effort while providing a native user experience.

In this chapter, we'll cover the following:

1. **What is Xamarin?**: Understand the basics of Xamarin and its components.
2. **Setting Up Xamarin**: Get started with Xamarin by setting up your development environment.
3. **Building a Simple To-Do List App**: Walk through a hands-on project where we'll create a to-do list mobile app that runs on both Android and iOS.
4. **Real-World Applications**: Explore how Xamarin can be used to build real-world apps, including examples from industries like healthcare, manufacturing, and logistics.

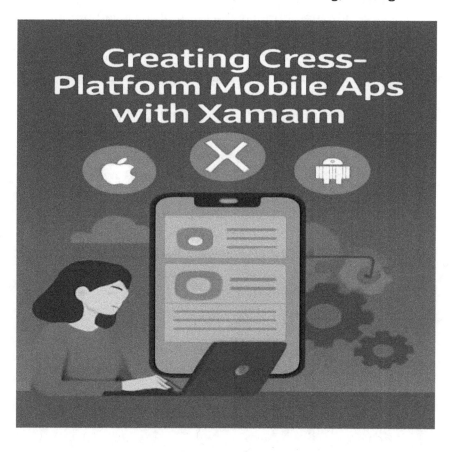

By the end of this chapter, you'll have a strong understanding of Xamarin and will be equipped to start building cross-platform mobile applications using C#.

What You'll Need

Software Requirements:

1. **Visual Studio:**
   - Visual Studio is the Integrated Development Environment (IDE) used for Xamarin development. It provides all the tools and components necessary to write, debug, and deploy Xamarin apps.
   - **Download:** You can download Visual Studio Community Edition from Visual Studio's website.
   - When installing Visual Studio, make sure to select the **Mobile Development with .NET** workload. This will install Xamarin and the necessary Android/iOS emulators.
2. **Xcode (for macOS users):**
   - If you're developing on macOS and want to target iOS, you will also need **Xcode**. It's the official IDE for building iOS apps.
   - **Download:** You can install Xcode from the Mac App Store.
3. **Android Studio (for Android emulation):**
   - Android Studio is used to emulate Android devices for testing your app.
   - **Download:** You can download Android Studio from the official website.

Hardware Requirements:

- A **laptop or desktop** with at least **8GB of RAM** and **4GB of available disk space** is recommended for smoother development.
- If you plan to deploy the app to physical Android or iOS devices for testing, you will need an Android or iOS device.

Prerequisites:

- **Basic C# Knowledge**: A fundamental understanding of C# is required, as Xamarin uses C# for writing mobile applications.
- **Basic Understanding of Mobile Development**: It would help if you had some basic understanding of mobile development concepts (such as user interfaces and interaction) before diving into Xamarin.

Chapter Overview

In this chapter, we will:

1. Understand what Xamarin is and how it enables cross-platform development.
2. Set up Xamarin and create a new mobile app project.
3. Build a simple **to-do list app** that runs on both Android and iOS using Xamarin.
4. Dive into real-world applications of Xamarin in various industries.

1. What is Xamarin?

Xamarin is a framework developed by **Microsoft** that allows developers to build cross-platform mobile applications using **C#** and **.NET**. Xamarin uses a single codebase to target both **Android** and **iOS** platforms, which means you don't have to write separate code for each platform.

How Xamarin Works

Xamarin allows you to write your app using C# and .NET, and it compiles the app into native code for Android and iOS. This means your app runs with the performance and functionality of a native app, but you only have to write your code once.

- **Xamarin.Forms**: A cross-platform UI toolkit that allows you to create shared user interfaces for both platforms.
- **Xamarin.iOS and Xamarin.Android**: These allow you to write platform-specific code if necessary (e.g., accessing native APIs for features that Xamarin.Forms doesn't support).

Benefits of Xamarin:

- **Single Codebase**: Write one set of code and deploy it to both Android and iOS.
- **Native Performance**: Xamarin provides access to native APIs, so you can build high-performance apps.
- **C# and .NET**: Xamarin uses C#, a language familiar to .NET developers, making it easier for C# developers to transition to mobile app development.
- **Access to Native Libraries**: Xamarin allows you to use native Android and iOS libraries when necessary.

- **Community and Support**: Xamarin is backed by Microsoft and has a large community of developers contributing to its growth.

---

2. Setting Up Xamarin

Before we begin building our app, let's set up Xamarin and ensure everything is ready for development.

Installing Xamarin in Visual Studio

1. **Download and Install Visual Studio**: If you haven't already, go to Visual Studio's download page and install the **Community Edition**. During installation, select the **Mobile Development with .NET** workload to install Xamarin.
2. **Install Android and iOS Emulators**: When you set up Xamarin, make sure to install the **Android Emulator** and **Xcode** (for iOS emulation on macOS). This will allow you to test your app in a virtual environment before deploying it to a physical device.
3. **Verify Your Installation**: Open Visual Studio and select **File > New Project > Mobile App (Xamarin.Forms)**. If you see this option, you've successfully installed Xamarin!

---

3. Building a Simple To-Do List App with Xamarin

Now that we have Xamarin set up, let's build a simple **to-do list app**. This app will allow users to add, view, and delete tasks. We will use **Xamarin.Forms** to create a cross-platform UI that works on both Android and iOS.

Step 1: Create a New Xamarin.Forms Project

1. Open **Visual Studio** and select **File > New Project**.
2. Select **Mobile App (Xamarin.Forms)** and click **Next**.
3. Choose the **Blank** template, which provides a simple starting point for our app.
4. Name your project **TodoApp** and click **Create**.

Step 2: Design the User Interface

Xamarin.Forms uses **XAML** to define the user interface. Let's start by creating a simple UI for our to-do list app.

1. In the **MainPage.xaml** file, replace the default code with the following:

```xml
<?xml version="1.0" encoding="utf-8" ?>
<ContentPage
xmlns="http://xamarin.com/schemas/2014/forms"

xmlns:x="http://schemas.microsoft.com/winfx/2006/xaml"
"
            x:Class="TodoApp.MainPage">
    <StackLayout Padding="20">
        <Label Text="To-Do List" FontSize="24"
HorizontalOptions="Center"/>
```

```
        <Entry x:Name="taskEntry" Placeholder="Enter
a task" />
        <Button Text="Add Task"
Clicked="OnAddTaskClicked"/>

        <ListView x:Name="taskListView"
ItemSelected="OnTaskSelected">
            <ListView.ItemTemplate>
                <DataTemplate>
                    <TextCell Text="{Binding Name}"
/>
                </DataTemplate>
            </ListView.ItemTemplate>
        </ListView>
    </StackLayout>
</ContentPage>
```

Explanation:

- We have a `Label` at the top that displays the title "To-Do List."
- An `Entry` control allows the user to type in a new task.
- A `Button` labeled "Add Task" triggers an event to add the task to a list.
- A `ListView` displays the list of tasks.

Step 3: Add Code Behind for Logic

In the **MainPage.xaml.cs** file, add the following logic to handle the task list operations:

csharp

```csharp
using System;
using System.Collections.ObjectModel;
using Xamarin.Forms;

namespace TodoApp
{
    public partial class MainPage : ContentPage
```

```csharp
    {
        public ObservableCollection<TaskItem> Tasks {
get; set; }

        public MainPage()
        {
            InitializeComponent();
            Tasks = new
ObservableCollection<TaskItem>();
            taskListView.ItemsSource = Tasks;
        }

        // Event handler for Add Task button
        private void OnAddTaskClicked(object sender,
EventArgs e)
        {
            if
(!string.IsNullOrEmpty(taskEntry.Text))
            {
                Tasks.Add(new TaskItem { Name =
taskEntry.Text });
                taskEntry.Text = string.Empty;  //
Clear the input
            }
        }

        // Event handler for task selection
        private void OnTaskSelected(object sender,
SelectedItemChangedEventArgs e)
        {
            if (e.SelectedItem != null)
            {
                var task = e.SelectedItem as
TaskItem;
                Tasks.Remove(task);  // Remove task
from list when selected
            }
        }
    }

    public class TaskItem
    {
        public string Name { get; set; }
    }
```

```
}
```

Explanation:

- **ObservableCollection<TaskItem> Tasks**: This is a collection that will hold the list of tasks. `ObservableCollection` automatically updates the UI when items are added or removed.
- **OnAddTaskClicked**: This method is triggered when the user clicks the "Add Task" button. It adds the task from the `Entry` field to the `Tasks` collection.
- **OnTaskSelected**: When a task is selected in the list, it is removed from the list, simulating the deletion of the task.

<u>Step 4: Test the App on Android and iOS Emulators</u>

1. **Run on Android Emulator**:
   - Click on the **Play** button in Visual Studio to build and deploy the app to the Android Emulator. You should see the to-do list app, where you can add tasks and remove them by selecting them from the list.
2. **Run on iOS Emulator** (macOS only):
   - If you're on macOS, you can run the app on the iOS simulator by selecting the iOS device in the dropdown and clicking **Play**.

4. Real-World Applications of Xamarin

Xamarin in Business-Critical Applications

While Xamarin is a great tool for developing games or simple apps, it is also widely used in **business-critical applications** across different industries. Here are some examples of how Xamarin is being used in real-world scenarios:

1. **Healthcare:**
   - Xamarin is used to develop **mobile health applications** that track patient data, monitor vital signs, and provide remote consultations.
   - Examples: Mobile apps that allow healthcare providers to monitor patients' health metrics in real time or manage appointments.
2. **Education:**
   - Many **educational apps** use Xamarin to provide interactive learning tools, quizzes, and educational videos for students.
   - Examples: Apps that provide course materials, track student progress, and allow communication between students and teachers.
3. **Manufacturing and Logistics:**
   - Xamarin is used to build apps that allow **real-time tracking of inventory, shipments, and assets**.
   - Examples: Apps for warehouse management, fleet tracking, and logistics coordination.
4. **E-Commerce:**
   - Xamarin is used in **shopping apps** that allow users to browse products, make payments, and track deliveries across platforms.

○ Examples: Apps that connect customers to online stores and payment gateways, providing a seamless shopping experience.

Conclusion

In this chapter, we explored **Xamarin,** a powerful framework for building cross-platform mobile applications with **C#.** You learned how to set up your development environment, create a simple **to-do list app,** and implement common mobile app features like adding and deleting tasks.

Xamarin's ability to share code between **Android** and **iOS** while maintaining native performance makes it an invaluable tool for mobile developers. By using Xamarin, you can streamline your development process and focus on building great features, rather than worrying about platform-specific code.

Whether you are building an e-commerce app, a healthcare solution, or a simple game, Xamarin provides the tools and flexibility you need to create high-quality mobile applications with a single codebase.

In the next chapter, we will explore **advanced Xamarin features**, such as integrating with native APIs, managing app lifecycle events, and optimizing app performance. Happy coding, and keep building!

Chapter 11: Advanced C# Concepts: Delegates, Events, and Lambdas

Introduction to Advanced C# Concepts

C# is a powerful, modern programming language that continues to evolve, offering a rich set of features that provide developers with a great deal of flexibility. Among these features are **delegates, events**, and **lambdas**—three advanced concepts that play a crucial role in enabling more dynamic, flexible, and efficient code.

In this chapter, we'll dive deep into these advanced concepts, understand how they work, and learn how to apply them effectively in real-world applications. These concepts are often used to implement event-driven programming, where different parts of the application can respond to user actions, system events, or other triggers.

We will also build a **dynamic event-driven application** that responds to user actions, allowing you to put your newfound knowledge to use in a real-world context.

What You'll Need

Before we start exploring these advanced C# concepts, let's ensure that you're set up to follow along with this chapter.

Software Requirements:

1. **Visual Studio:**
   - Visual Studio is the primary IDE for C# development. It includes all the tools and features needed to write, debug, and run C# code.
   - **Download:** You can download **Visual Studio Community Edition** from Visual Studio's website.
2. **.NET SDK:**
   - You'll need the **.NET SDK** to develop and run C# applications. This will ensure you have access to the latest features and libraries.
   - **Download:** You can download the .NET SDK from Microsoft's official .NET page.
3. **Windows, macOS, or Linux:**
   - C# and .NET can run on all major operating systems, so you can develop and run your code on Windows, macOS, or Linux.

Hardware Requirements:

- A **computer** with at least **4GB of RAM** is recommended. More memory and processing power will help when running larger applications, especially when working with real-time systems or multiple events.

Prerequisites:

- **Basic C# Knowledge**: A fundamental understanding of C# syntax and object-oriented programming (OOP) is required. If you're not familiar with the basics of C#, review the earlier chapters before starting this one.
- **Understanding of Methods**: You should be comfortable working with methods in C# (e.g., creating, calling, and passing parameters to them).

Chapter Overview

In this chapter, we will:

1. **Understand Delegates**: Learn how delegates work and how they enable dynamic method invocation.
2. **Explore Events**: Understand how events build on delegates to facilitate event-driven programming in C#.
3. **Master Lambdas**: Discover the power of **lambda expressions**, which provide a concise way to write inline functions.
4. **Hands-On Project**: We'll build a **dynamic event-driven application** that responds to user actions, such as clicking buttons or other interactions.
5. **Real-World Applications**: Learn how these concepts can be applied to real-world applications, such as **stock trading apps** or **live monitoring systems**.

1. Understanding Delegates

What is a Delegate?

In C#, a **delegate** is a type-safe method pointer, meaning it points to a method that has a specific signature. Think of a delegate as a **contract** that ensures a method conforms to a certain signature (parameters and return type). Delegates allow methods to be passed as parameters, making your code more flexible.

Delegates are widely used in scenarios such as:

- **Callback functions**: Passing a method as an argument and executing it later.
- **Event handling**: Used to attach methods to events (which we'll cover in the next section).

How Delegates Work

Let's start by defining a simple delegate and using it to call a method.

```csharp
using System;

public class Program
{
    // Define a delegate type
    public delegate void MyDelegate(string message);

    static void Main(string[] args)
    {
        // Create an instance of the delegate,
pointing to the PrintMessage method
        MyDelegate del = PrintMessage;
```

```
        // Invoke the delegate
        del("Hello from delegate!");
    }

    // Method that matches the delegate's signature
    static void PrintMessage(string message)
    {
        Console.WriteLine(message);
    }
}
```

Explanation:

- **MyDelegate:** This defines the delegate type that takes a string parameter and returns void.
- We assign the PrintMessage method to the del delegate and then call del() to invoke it.

Multicast Delegates

One of the most powerful features of delegates is the ability to create **multicast delegates**. A multicast delegate can reference multiple methods, allowing all methods to be invoked when the delegate is called.

```csharp
public delegate void MyDelegate(string message);

public class Program
{
    static void Main(string[] args)
    {
        MyDelegate del = PrintMessage;
        del += PrintMessageUpperCase;   // Add another
method to the delegate chain

        del("Hello, world!");   // Both methods will
be called
    }
```

```
static void PrintMessage(string message)
{
    Console.WriteLine(message);
}

static void PrintMessageUpperCase(string message)
{
    Console.WriteLine(message.ToUpper());
}
}
```

Explanation:

- **del += PrintMessageUpperCase:** This adds another method (PrintMessageUpperCase) to the delegate chain.
- When the delegate is invoked, both methods are called in the order they were added.

2. Understanding Events

What is an Event?

An **event** in C# is a special kind of delegate. It is a mechanism that allows an object to **notify other objects** when something of interest happens. Events are used to implement the **observer pattern**, where one object (the publisher) sends notifications to other objects (the subscribers).

In simpler terms, an event is a way for a class to broadcast notifications to other classes when certain actions or changes occur.

Event Declaration and Handling

An event is declared using the `event` keyword, and event handlers (methods that respond to the event) are associated with it using a delegate.

Here's an example that demonstrates how to use events:

```csharp
using System;

public class Publisher
{
    // Declare an event using a delegate
    public event Action<string> Notify;

    public void TriggerEvent(string message)
    {
        // Trigger the event
        Notify?.Invoke(message);
    }
}

public class Subscriber
{
    public void Subscribe(Publisher publisher)
    {
        // Subscribe to the event
        publisher.Notify += OnEventTriggered;
    }

    // Event handler
    private void OnEventTriggered(string message)
    {
        Console.WriteLine("Event received: " +
message);
    }
}

public class Program
{
```

```
static void Main(string[] args)
{
    Publisher publisher = new Publisher();
    Subscriber subscriber = new Subscriber();

    // Subscribe to the event
    subscriber.Subscribe(publisher);

    // Trigger the event
    publisher.TriggerEvent("Hello, World!");
}
}
```

Explanation:

- The `Publisher` class defines an event (`Notify`) using a delegate (`Action<string>`).
- The `Subscriber` class subscribes to the event and defines an event handler (`OnEventTriggered`) to respond when the event is triggered.
- When `publisher.TriggerEvent()` is called, the event is triggered, and the `OnEventTriggered` method in the subscriber is executed.

---

3. Working with Lambdas

What is a Lambda Expression?

A **lambda expression** is a concise way of writing inline functions or delegates. Lambdas provide a shorthand syntax for defining anonymous methods and are frequently used in conjunction with LINQ, delegates, and events.

The basic syntax of a lambda expression is:

csharp

```
(parameter list) => expression
```

For example:

csharp

```
Func<int, int, int> add = (x, y) => x + y;
Console.WriteLine(add(2, 3));   // Output: 5
```

In this example, the lambda expression `(x, y) => x + y` defines a simple function that adds two numbers. The lambda is assigned to the `add` delegate, which is then invoked with `add(2, 3)`.

Lambdas with Delegates and Events

Lambdas are often used with delegates and events to define quick, inline methods. Here's an example that uses a lambda expression with an event:

csharp

```
using System;

public class Publisher
{
    public event Action<string> Notify;

    public void TriggerEvent(string message)
    {
        Notify?.Invoke(message);
    }
}

public class Program
{
    static void Main(string[] args)
    {
        Publisher publisher = new Publisher();
```

```
        // Subscribe to the event using a lambda
        publisher.Notify += (message) =>
Console.WriteLine("Event received: " + message);

        // Trigger the event
        publisher.TriggerEvent("Hello, Lambda!");
    }
}
```

Explanation:

- We use a lambda expression `(message) => Console.WriteLine(...)` to subscribe to the `Notify` event and define the event handler inline.
- When the event is triggered, the lambda expression is executed.

---

4. Hands-On Project: Dynamic Event-Driven Application

Now that we understand delegates, events, and lambdas, let's build a **dynamic event-driven application** that responds to user actions. This app will simulate a **stock price monitoring system** where users can subscribe to stock price updates and receive notifications when the price changes.

Step 1: Define the Event and Delegate

First, let's create a `StockPricePublisher` class that will raise an event whenever the stock price changes.

csharp

```
using System;
```

```
public class StockPricePublisher
{
    public event Action<string> PriceChanged;

    public void ChangePrice(string stockName, double
newPrice)
    {
        // Simulate price change
        Console.WriteLine($"{stockName} price changed
to {newPrice}");

        // Raise the event
        PriceChanged?.Invoke($"{stockName} price
updated to {newPrice}");
    }
}
```

Step 2: Define the Subscriber

Next, we'll create a `StockPriceSubscriber` class that will subscribe to the event and display the updated stock prices.

csharp

```
public class StockPriceSubscriber
{
    public void Subscribe(StockPricePublisher
publisher)
    {
        publisher.PriceChanged += OnPriceChanged;
    }

    private void OnPriceChanged(string message)
    {
        Console.WriteLine($"Notification:
{message}");
    }
}
```

Step 3: Implement the Main Program

In the `Program.cs` file, implement the main application logic.

csharp

```csharp
public class Program
{
    static void Main(string[] args)
    {
        // Create publisher and subscriber
        StockPricePublisher publisher = new
StockPricePublisher();
        StockPriceSubscriber subscriber = new
StockPriceSubscriber();

        // Subscribe to the price change event
        subscriber.Subscribe(publisher);

        // Simulate stock price changes
        publisher.ChangePrice("AAPL", 150.75);
        publisher.ChangePrice("GOOG", 2800.50);
    }
}
```

Step 4: Test the Application

Run the application, and you should see the following output:

vbnet

```
AAPL price changed to 150.75
Notification: AAPL price updated to 150.75
GOOG price changed to 2800.5
Notification: GOOG price updated to 2800.5
```

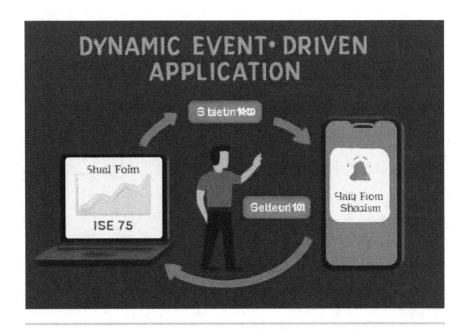

5. Real-World Application: Event-Driven Programming

Real-Time Stock Trading Apps

In stock trading apps, real-time price updates are critical. Events and delegates are used extensively to notify users about price changes, order executions, and news alerts. When you subscribe to stock prices in a real trading app, the system triggers events every time the price updates, providing users with the most current information without having to refresh the app.

Live Monitoring Systems

In industries like healthcare or manufacturing, **live monitoring systems** track various metrics (e.g., heart rate, machine performance). These systems rely heavily on event-driven programming, where system components react to real-time events, such as a sudden change in data. By using delegates, events, and lambdas, developers can create efficient systems that process and respond to real-time data.

Conclusion

In this chapter, we explored advanced C# concepts—**delegates**, **events**, and **lambdas**—which are essential for writing flexible, event-driven applications. You learned how delegates enable dynamic method invocation, how events provide a way for objects to notify others of changes, and how lambdas allow for concise, inline methods.

By building a **stock price monitoring system**, you gained hands-on experience with event-driven programming. These concepts are invaluable in building real-time applications, such as **stock trading apps** or **live monitoring systems**, where quick reactions to events are critical.

In the next chapter, we will dive into **asynchronous programming** with `async` and `await`, allowing you to perform tasks concurrently without blocking your application's UI.

Chapter 12: Real-Time Applications with SignalR

Introduction to Real-Time Communication

In modern applications, real-time communication between the server and client is becoming an essential feature. Imagine chatting with friends on a messaging app, receiving instant updates on your stock portfolio, or playing an online game where your movements are synchronized with other players—all in real-time. This level of interactivity requires seamless communication, where data is pushed from the server to the client instantly as events happen.

This is where **SignalR** comes in.

SignalR is a powerful library in ASP.NET that simplifies the process of adding real-time functionality to web applications. It allows the server to push content to clients in real-time, meaning that the clients don't have to keep asking the server for new data. Instead, the server pushes updates to the clients as soon as something changes.

In this chapter, we will explore how to build **real-time applications** using SignalR, focusing on its capabilities to enable real-time communication. We will build a **real-time chat application** as our hands-on project, and then discuss real-world applications of SignalR, such as **customer support systems**, **chatbots**, and **multiplayer games**.

By the end of this chapter, you will have a deep understanding of SignalR and how to use it to create dynamic, interactive applications.

What You'll Need

Software Requirements:

1. **Visual Studio:**
   - Visual Studio is the most commonly used IDE for developing .NET applications. It provides powerful features like debugging, syntax highlighting, and integrated tools for SignalR development.
   - **Download**: You can download **Visual Studio Community Edition** from Visual Studio's website.
2. **.NET SDK:**
   - The **.NET SDK** is required to run and develop .NET Core applications. It is necessary for building and running SignalR applications.
   - **Download**: You can download the .NET SDK from Microsoft's .NET download page.
3. **Browser:**
   - A modern browser (Google Chrome, Firefox, etc.) will be needed to run the real-time application.

Hardware Requirements:

- **Computer:** A **laptop or desktop** with at least **4GB of RAM** is recommended for smoother development.

<u>Prerequisites:</u>

- **Basic C# Knowledge**: A basic understanding of C# programming concepts (e.g., classes, methods, and basic event handling) is required.
- **Basic Web Development**: Familiarity with HTML, CSS, and JavaScript will be helpful but not required.

Chapter Overview

In this chapter, we will:

1. **Understand SignalR**: Learn what SignalR is and how it works, including its underlying technology.
2. **Set Up SignalR in a Project**: Set up SignalR in an ASP.NET Core application.
3. **Build a Real-Time Chat Application**: Walk through building a real-time chat app using SignalR, where users can send messages that are instantly received by all connected clients.
4. **Real-World Applications of SignalR**: Explore how SignalR is used in real-world scenarios, including customer support, multiplayer games, and chatbots.

1. Understanding SignalR

<u>What is SignalR?</u>

SignalR is a **real-time communication library** for ASP.NET that allows you to add real-time functionality to your applications.

With SignalR, your server-side code can send asynchronous notifications to client-side web applications.

In traditional web applications, the client (e.g., a browser) sends HTTP requests to the server to get data (such as when you reload a webpage). However, with real-time applications, the server can push data to the client without the client having to request it.

Key Features of SignalR:

1. **Real-time Communication**: SignalR enables full-duplex communication, meaning the server can send messages to clients at any time without waiting for a request.
2. **Persistent Connections**: SignalR uses persistent connections, meaning a client can remain connected to the server throughout the lifecycle of the app.
3. **Automatic Reconnection**: SignalR handles automatic reconnection when the connection between the client and server is lost.
4. **Scalability**: SignalR can scale with the use of **SignalR Hubs** and can be integrated with cloud-based services like Azure to handle large numbers of connections.
5. **Transport Mechanisms**: SignalR automatically selects the best transport method available, such as **WebSockets, Server-Sent Events**, or **Long Polling**, based on the client's capabilities.

How SignalR Works

SignalR operates based on **hubs**, which are high-level abstractions that simplify the process of managing connections, broadcasting messages, and handling events.

- **Clients** connect to **SignalR hubs**.
- **Server-side code** sends messages to **client-side code** via the hubs.
- **Client-side code** receives the messages and reacts to them (e.g., updating the UI in real-time).

---

2. Setting Up SignalR in a Project

To start using SignalR in your application, we need to install the necessary libraries and set up SignalR in the project.

Step 1: Create a New ASP.NET Core Project

1. Open **Visual Studio** and create a new **ASP.NET Core Web Application**.
2. Choose the **Web Application (Model-View-Controller)** template.
3. Name your project (e.g., **RealTimeChatApp**) and click **Create**.

Step 2: Install SignalR Package

SignalR is not included by default in the ASP.NET Core templates, so we need to install the **SignalR** NuGet package.

1. Right-click on your project and select **Manage NuGet Packages**.
2. In the **Browse** tab, search for **Microsoft.AspNetCore.SignalR** and install it.

Alternatively, you can install it via the **Package Manager Console**:

```bash
Install-Package Microsoft.AspNetCore.SignalR
```

Step 3: Configure SignalR in Startup.cs

In the `Startup.cs` file, configure SignalR by adding it to the `ConfigureServices` method and setting up the routing in the `Configure` method.

```csharp
public class Startup
{
    public void ConfigureServices(IServiceCollection services)
    {
        services.AddSignalR(); // Register SignalR services
    }

    public void Configure(IApplicationBuilder app, IWebHostEnvironment env)
    {
        if (env.IsDevelopment())
        {
            app.UseDeveloperExceptionPage();
        }

        app.UseRouting();

        app.UseEndpoints(endpoints =>
        {
            endpoints.MapHub<ChatHub>("/chatHub"); // Map the SignalR hub to a route
        });
    }
}
```

In this code:

- **AddSignalR()** registers the SignalR services with the ASP.NET Core dependency injection system.
- **MapHub<ChatHub>("/chatHub")** maps the SignalR hub to the /chatHub route. This is where clients will connect.

3. Building a Real-Time Chat Application

Now, let's build a simple **real-time chat application** using SignalR. This app will allow users to send and receive messages in real-time.

Step 1: Create the SignalR Hub

A **hub** is a class that handles communication between the client and the server. We will create a ChatHub class that manages the messaging between clients.

Create a new class called ChatHub.cs in the **Hubs** folder:

```csharp
using Microsoft.AspNetCore.SignalR;

public class ChatHub : Hub
{
    // Send a message to all connected clients
    public async Task SendMessage(string user, string message)
    {
        await Clients.All.SendAsync("ReceiveMessage", user, message);  // Sends the message to all clients
    }
}
```

Explanation:

- The `SendMessage` method takes the `user` and `message` as parameters and broadcasts them to all connected clients using the `Clients.All.SendAsync` method.
- The `ReceiveMessage` method will be triggered on the client side when a message is received.

Step 2: Create the Front-End (Client-Side)

Now, let's build the client-side part of the app, which will allow users to send and receive messages.

1. Open the `Views/Home/Index.cshtml` file and replace it with the following code:

html

```html
@{
    ViewData["Title"] = "Real-Time Chat";
}

<h1>@ViewData["Title"]</h1>

<div>
    <input id="userInput" type="text"
placeholder="Enter your name" />
    <textarea id="messageInput" placeholder="Enter
your message"></textarea>
    <button id="sendButton">Send</button>
</div>

<div id="chatBox">
    <ul id="messagesList"></ul>
</div>

@section Scripts {
    <script
src="https://cdnjs.cloudflare.com/ajax/libs/microsoft
-signalr/5.0.8/signalr.min.js"></script>
    <script>
        // Establish connection with SignalR hub
```

```
        const connection = new
signalR.HubConnectionBuilder().withUrl("/chatHub").bu
ild();

        // Receive messages from the server
        connection.on("ReceiveMessage", (user,
message) => {
            const messageElement =
document.createElement("li");
            messageElement.textContent = `${user}:
${message}`;

document.getElementById("messagesList").appendChild(m
essageElement);
        });

        // Start connection
        connection.start().catch(err =>
console.error(err));

        // Send a message when the button is clicked

document.getElementById("sendButton").addEventListene
r("click", () => {
            const user =
document.getElementById("userInput").value;
            const message =
document.getElementById("messageInput").value;
            connection.invoke("SendMessage", user,
message).catch(err => console.error(err));
        });
    </script>
}
```

Explanation:

- **connection.on("ReceiveMessage", ...)**: This listens for messages from the server and adds them to the #messagesList element.

- **connection.invoke("SendMessage", user, message):** This sends a message to the server when the "Send" button is clicked.
- **connection.start():** Starts the connection to the SignalR hub.

Step 3: Test the Application

1. Press **F5** or **Ctrl + F5** to run the application.
2. Open multiple browser windows and navigate to `http://localhost:5000` to test the real-time chat functionality.
3. Enter a name and message in one window, click **Send,** and the message will appear in all other open windows in real-time.

---

4. Real-World Applications of SignalR

Real-Time Messaging Systems

SignalR is widely used in **real-time messaging systems,** such as:

- **Customer support chat:** Where support agents and customers can communicate instantly.
- **Chatbots:** For building intelligent systems that respond to customer inquiries in real-time.
- **Multiplayer games:** For syncing players' actions in real-time, such as in first-person shooters or online strategy games.

Stock Trading and Monitoring Systems

SignalR is ideal for building **stock trading** platforms where prices are constantly updated in real-time. Traders need to receive immediate updates as stock prices change. With SignalR, the server can push updates to all connected clients, ensuring they have the most current information.

Healthcare Monitoring Systems

In healthcare, **real-time monitoring systems** allow doctors and nurses to get live updates on patients' vital signs. SignalR can be used to transmit patient data from monitoring equipment to healthcare professionals in real-time, enabling immediate action when necessary.

Conclusion

In this chapter, we explored the fundamentals of **SignalR** and how it enables real-time communication between servers and clients. You learned how to set up a SignalR hub, create real-time interactions in a chat application, and understood the underlying concepts of real-time communication.

SignalR is a powerful tool that allows you to build dynamic, interactive applications with minimal effort. By leveraging SignalR in real-world applications such as **real-time messaging, multiplayer gaming**, and **stock trading**, you can create more engaging and efficient user experiences.

In the next chapter, we will explore **advanced SignalR features**, including scaling SignalR applications, handling group communication, and integrating SignalR with other technologies like **SignalR with Angular**. Keep experimenting with SignalR, and happy coding!

Chapter 13: Database Integration with C#

Introduction to Database Integration with C#

In software development, managing and interacting with databases is a core component of many applications. From storing user data to keeping track of transactions or maintaining inventory, databases are where the data lives and evolves. Integrating databases into your C# applications is essential for building dynamic, data-driven solutions that can scale and handle complex operations.

In this chapter, we will explore how to integrate both **SQL** and **NoSQL** databases with C# applications. You'll learn how to interact with databases, execute queries, and manage data storage in different types of databases. This chapter is designed to help you integrate database functionality into your applications seamlessly, whether you are building a finance app, a healthcare solution, or a logistics system.

We will walk through a hands-on project where we create an app to track **user purchases**, save the data to a **local database**, and display the purchase history. By the end of this chapter, you will understand how to interact with databases in C#, work with both SQL and NoSQL databases, and apply these techniques to real-world scenarios.

What You'll Need

Software Requirements:

1. **Visual Studio**:
   - **Visual Studio** is the IDE used for building C# applications. It provides all the tools you need for coding, debugging, and testing. Make sure to install **Visual Studio Community Edition** and the **.NET Core SDK**.
   - **Download**: Visual Studio Download
2. **SQL Server**:
   - For **SQL Database integration**, you will need **SQL Server** or **SQL Server Express** installed on your machine. SQL Server is a powerful relational database management system (RDBMS) used by many enterprises to store and manage data.
   - **Download**: SQL Server Express
3. **MongoDB** (For NoSQL integration):
   - For **NoSQL Database integration**, we will use **MongoDB**, a NoSQL database that stores data in flexible, JSON-like documents.
   - **Download**: MongoDB Download
4. **.NET Entity Framework (EF Core)**:
   - Entity Framework Core (EF Core) is an Object-Relational Mapping (ORM) framework that allows you to interact with databases using C# objects.
   - **Install**: Use NuGet to install **Microsoft.EntityFrameworkCore** in your C# project for SQL database integration.
5. **MongoDB Driver for C#**:
   - To work with MongoDB, you will need the **MongoDB driver for C#**.

   o   **Install**: Use NuGet to install **MongoDB.Driver** in your C# project.

Hardware Requirements:

- A **laptop or desktop** with at least **4GB of RAM** for smooth performance.
- A **local or remote database** setup where you can store and retrieve data. You can use cloud solutions (e.g., Azure, AWS) if you prefer not to install databases locally.

Prerequisites:

- **Basic C# Knowledge**: You should be comfortable with basic C# concepts, including data types, variables, and object-oriented programming (OOP).
- **Basic Database Concepts**: Familiarity with basic database concepts like tables, rows, and queries will help. If you're new to databases, don't worry—we'll guide you through the essentials as we go.

Chapter Overview

In this chapter, we will:

1. **Understand Database Integration**: Learn how to connect to databases, run queries, and manage data in both SQL and NoSQL databases.
2. **SQL Integration with C#**: Set up and connect to an SQL database using **Entity Framework Core** and perform CRUD operations.

3. **NoSQL Integration with C#**: Set up and connect to **MongoDB** and perform data operations.
4. **Hands-On Project**: Build an app to track **user purchases**, save them to a **local database**, and display the purchase history.
5. **Real-World Applications**: Learn how database integration is used in real-world applications like **finance, healthcare**, and **logistics**.

---

1. Understanding Database Integration with C#

What is Database Integration?

Database integration is the process of connecting your application to a database and interacting with it. Your application can read data from the database, store new data, and update or delete existing records. There are two main types of databases you'll work with in C# development:

- **SQL Databases**: These are relational databases that use Structured Query Language (SQL) to manage data. Examples include **SQL Server, MySQL**, and **PostgreSQL**.
- **NoSQL Databases**: These are non-relational databases that store data in flexible formats like JSON. Examples include **MongoDB, Cassandra**, and **Redis**.

Why Use Databases in C# Applications?

1. **Persistent Storage**: Databases provide a reliable way to store data persistently, meaning the data remains intact even after the application is closed.
2. **Data Retrieval**: Databases allow you to retrieve data efficiently using queries, making it easy to display user data or analyze records.
3. **Scalability**: As your application grows, databases provide a scalable solution to handle larger amounts of data and higher traffic.
4. **Security**: Databases provide built-in features to secure data and manage access control.

---

2. SQL Database Integration with C#

Setting Up a SQL Database

To begin, let's set up a **SQL Server** instance (either locally or in the cloud) and create a **simple database** to store user purchase data.

1. **Create a Database in SQL Server:**
   - Open **SQL Server Management Studio** (SSMS).
   - Right-click on **Databases** and select **New Database.**
   - Name the database `PurchaseTracker`.
2. **Create a Table:**
   - In the `PurchaseTracker` database, create a table called `Purchases` with the following columns:
     - `Id` (INT, Primary Key, Identity)
     - `UserName` (VARCHAR)
     - `Product` (VARCHAR)

- Amount **(DECIMAL)**
- PurchaseDate **(DATETIME)**

sql

```
CREATE TABLE Purchases (
    Id INT PRIMARY KEY IDENTITY(1,1),
    UserName VARCHAR(100),
    Product VARCHAR(100),
    Amount DECIMAL(18, 2),
    PurchaseDate DATETIME
);
```

Integrating with Entity Framework Core

We'll use **Entity Framework Core (EF Core)**, which allows us to interact with the database using C# objects rather than writing raw SQL queries. EF Core maps C# classes to database tables and provides methods to perform CRUD operations.

Step 1: Create a C# Model Class

In your C# project, create a class called `Purchase` that will map to the `Purchases` table in the database:

csharp

```
public class Purchase
{
    public int Id { get; set; }
    public string UserName { get; set; }
    public string Product { get; set; }
    public decimal Amount { get; set; }
    public DateTime PurchaseDate { get; set; }
}
```

Step 2: Set Up the DbContext

Create a `PurchaseDbContext` class that inherits from `DbContext`. This class will manage the connection to the SQL Server database.

csharp

```csharp
using Microsoft.EntityFrameworkCore;

public class PurchaseDbContext : DbContext
{
    public DbSet<Purchase> Purchases { get; set; }

    protected override void
OnConfiguring(DbContextOptionsBuilder optionsBuilder)
    {

optionsBuilder.UseSqlServer("Server=localhost;Databas
e=PurchaseTracker;Trusted_Connection=True;");
    }
}
```

Explanation:

- `DbSet<Purchase>` represents the `Purchases` table in the database.
- `OnConfiguring` method sets the connection string to the SQL Server instance.

Step 3: Perform CRUD Operations

Now that we've set up the database context, let's perform some basic **CRUD** operations.

1. **Create** a new purchase and add it to the database:

csharp

```csharp
using (var context = new PurchaseDbContext())
{
    var newPurchase = new Purchase
    {
        UserName = "John Doe",
        Product = "Laptop",
        Amount = 999.99M,
        PurchaseDate = DateTime.Now
    };
    context.Purchases.Add(newPurchase);
    context.SaveChanges();
}
```

2. **Read** all purchases from the database:

csharp

```csharp
using (var context = new PurchaseDbContext())
{
    var purchases = context.Purchases.ToList();
    foreach (var purchase in purchases)
    {
        Console.WriteLine($"User:
{purchase.UserName}, Product: {purchase.Product},
Amount: {purchase.Amount}");
    }
}
```

3. **Update** a purchase:

csharp

```csharp
using (var context = new PurchaseDbContext())
{
    var purchase = context.Purchases.FirstOrDefault(p
=> p.Id == 1);
    if (purchase != null)
    {
        purchase.Amount = 950.00M;
        context.SaveChanges();
    }
```

}

4. **Delete** a purchase:

```csharp
using (var context = new PurchaseDbContext())
{
    var purchase = context.Purchases.FirstOrDefault(p
=> p.Id == 1);
    if (purchase != null)
    {
        context.Purchases.Remove(purchase);
        context.SaveChanges();
    }
}
```

Step 4: Testing the Application

Run the application and test the CRUD operations. You should be able to create, read, update, and delete purchase records in the SQL database using EF Core.

---

3. NoSQL Database Integration with C#

In addition to SQL databases, many modern applications also use **NoSQL databases**, which are more flexible and scalable, especially for unstructured data.

Setting Up MongoDB

Let's set up a **MongoDB** database and use it with C# for handling user purchase data.

1. **Install MongoDB:**

- o Download and install **MongoDB** from the official MongoDB website.
  - o Start the MongoDB server by running `mongod` in the command prompt.
2. **Create a Database and Collection**:
  - o Open **MongoDB Compass** (or use the MongoDB shell) and create a new database called `PurchaseTracker` and a collection called `Purchases`.

Integrating MongoDB with C#

To interact with MongoDB, we will use the **MongoDB.Driver** library. You can install this via NuGet:

bash

```
Install-Package MongoDB.Driver
```

Step 1: Create a C# Model Class

The model for MongoDB will look similar to the SQL model:

csharp

```
public class Purchase
{
    public ObjectId Id { get; set; }
    public string UserName { get; set; }
    public string Product { get; set; }
    public decimal Amount { get; set; }
    public DateTime PurchaseDate { get; set; }
}
```

Step 2: Set Up MongoDB Client

Now, let's connect to MongoDB using the `MongoClient` class:

csharp

```
using MongoDB.Driver;

public class PurchaseRepository
{
    private readonly IMongoCollection<Purchase>
_purchases;

    public PurchaseRepository()
    {
        var client = new
MongoClient("mongodb://localhost:27017");
        var database =
client.GetDatabase("PurchaseTracker");
        _purchases =
database.GetCollection<Purchase>("Purchases");
    }

    public void AddPurchase(Purchase purchase)
    {
        _purchases.InsertOne(purchase);
    }

    public List<Purchase> GetPurchases()
    {
        return _purchases.Find(p => true).ToList();
    }
}
```

Explanation:

- `MongoClient` connects to the MongoDB instance.
- `GetDatabase("PurchaseTracker")` connects to the `PurchaseTracker` database.
- `GetCollection<Purchase>("Purchases")` retrieves the `Purchases` collection.

Step 3: Perform CRUD Operations

1. **Create** a new purchase:

```csharp
csharp
```

```csharp
var purchase = new Purchase
{
    UserName = "Jane Doe",
    Product = "Smartphone",
    Amount = 799.99M,
    PurchaseDate = DateTime.Now
};
var repo = new PurchaseRepository();
repo.AddPurchase(purchase);
```

2. **Read** all purchases:

```csharp
csharp
```

```csharp
var purchases = repo.GetPurchases();
foreach (var purchase in purchases)
{
    Console.WriteLine($"User: {purchase.UserName},
Product: {purchase.Product}, Amount:
{purchase.Amount}");
}
```

3. **Update** a purchase:

```csharp
csharp
```

```csharp
var updateFilter = Builders<Purchase>.Filter.Eq(p =>
p.UserName, "Jane Doe");
var update = Builders<Purchase>.Update.Set(p =>
p.Amount, 750.00M);
repo._purchases.UpdateOne(updateFilter, update);
```

4. **Delete** a purchase:

```csharp
csharp
```

```csharp
var deleteFilter = Builders<Purchase>.Filter.Eq(p =>
p.UserName, "Jane Doe");
repo._purchases.DeleteOne(deleteFilter);
```

4. Real-World Applications of Database Integration

Finance:

In finance applications, databases are used to store transaction data, track investments, and generate reports. **SQL databases** are often used for their ability to handle complex queries and relationships between data (e.g., customers, transactions, investments).

Example: A banking app that tracks account balances, records transactions, and generates monthly statements.

Healthcare:

In healthcare applications, databases store patient information, medical records, prescriptions, and more. **NoSQL databases**, like MongoDB, are often used in healthcare apps due to their flexibility in handling unstructured data (e.g., patient notes, diagnostic images).

Example: A healthcare system that allows doctors to track patient visits, prescriptions, and medical histories.

Logistics:

In logistics applications, databases are used to manage inventory, shipping records, and warehouse data. **SQL databases** are commonly used to track goods, whereas **NoSQL databases** are employed for real-time inventory updates.

Example: A logistics system that tracks the shipment status and inventory levels across different warehouses.

Conclusion

In this chapter, we explored how to integrate both **SQL** and **NoSQL** databases into C# applications. You learned how to use **Entity Framework Core** to interact with SQL databases like SQL Server and how to use **MongoDB** for NoSQL storage. We also built a simple application to track user purchases, saving data to both SQL and NoSQL databases.

By mastering database integration, you can build dynamic, data-driven applications that support a wide range of use cases in industries like **finance, healthcare**, and **logistics**. In the next chapter, we will explore **advanced data handling techniques**, including **data migrations**, **optimizing queries**, and **working with large datasets**.

Keep experimenting with databases, and happy coding!

Chapter 14: Debugging and Troubleshooting in C#

Introduction to Debugging and Troubleshooting

As a developer, encountering bugs is an inevitable part of the software development process. Debugging and troubleshooting are vital skills that every programmer needs to master to identify, fix, and prevent issues in code. These skills are not only about fixing the immediate problems but also about improving the overall quality and maintainability of the code.

In this chapter, we will dive into **debugging tools in Visual Studio**, the **best practices for troubleshooting**, and how to use various techniques to diagnose and fix bugs in your C# applications. We will guide you through an engaging **hands-on project**, where we will intentionally introduce bugs into an application, and you'll use the Visual Studio debugging tools to track them down and fix them.

By the end of this chapter, you will have a thorough understanding of how to use debugging tools, such as **breakpoints, watches, the console**, and more, to make your coding process more efficient and ensure that your applications are bug-free.

What You'll Need

Software Requirements:

1. **Visual Studio:**
   - Visual Studio is the most commonly used IDE for C# development. It has built-in tools that make debugging easier, such as **breakpoints, watch windows**, and **call stacks**.
   - **Download**: You can download **Visual Studio Community Edition** from Visual Studio's website.
2. **.NET SDK:**
   - The **.NET SDK** is required for compiling and running C# applications. Make sure you have the SDK installed.
   - **Download**: You can download the .NET SDK from Microsoft's .NET page.

Hardware Requirements:

- A **laptop or desktop** with **4GB of RAM** is recommended, although more powerful hardware will help with larger applications.

Prerequisites:

- **Basic C# Knowledge**: You should be comfortable with basic C# syntax and concepts like variables, methods, and control flow.
- **Familiarity with Visual Studio**: While we'll walk through the tools in Visual Studio, it's helpful to have some prior experience with the IDE.

Chapter Overview

In this chapter, we will:

1. **Learn Debugging Tools**: Understand how to use breakpoints, watches, and the console in Visual Studio.
2. **Best Practices for Troubleshooting**: Learn effective strategies for identifying and resolving issues in your code.
3. **Hands-On Project**: Debug an application that contains intentional bugs, using Visual Studio's debugging tools to fix them.
4. **Real-World Application**: Understand how to apply debugging and troubleshooting techniques to production-level code in industries like **finance**, **healthcare**, and **logistics**.

1. Understanding Debugging Tools in Visual Studio

What is Debugging?

Debugging is the process of identifying and fixing bugs or errors in a program. It involves examining code execution, monitoring variables, and tracking the flow of the application to uncover why certain behaviors occur. **Visual Studio** provides a variety of tools to help developers debug their code efficiently.

Visual Studio Debugging Tools

Breakpoints

A **breakpoint** is a marker that tells the debugger to pause the execution of your code at a specific line, allowing you to inspect the program's state.

1. **How to Set a Breakpoint**:
    - To set a breakpoint, click on the **left margin** next to the line number where you want to pause execution. A red dot will appear, indicating that a breakpoint has been set.
    - When the program execution reaches this line, it will pause, allowing you to inspect variables, step through the code, or analyze the call stack.
2. **Using Breakpoints in Action**:
    - Let's consider the following example of a simple calculator application:

```csharp
public class Calculator
{
    public int Add(int a, int b)
    {
        int result = a + b;
        return result;
    }

    public int Multiply(int a, int b)
    {
        int result = a * b;
        return result;
    }
}
```

- Set a breakpoint at the line where the `result` variable is assigned. When running the program, execution will pause, and you can inspect the values of `a`, `b`, and `result` at that moment.

3. **Breakpoints Window**:
   o You can view and manage all breakpoints in Visual Studio by opening the **Breakpoints Window** (found in **Debug > Windows > Breakpoints**). This window allows you to enable, disable, and delete breakpoints.

Watches

A **watch** is a tool that allows you to monitor the value of a variable or expression while the program is running.

1. **How to Add a Watch**:
   o Right-click a variable or expression during a debugging session, and select **Add Watch**. Alternatively, open the **Watch Window** from **Debug > Windows > Watch > Watch 1**.
   o This will display the current value of the variable or expression as the program executes.
2. **Practical Example**:
   o In the calculator application, you can add a watch for the `result` variable. While debugging, Visual Studio will display its current value and update it in real-time as you step through the code.

Immediate Window

The **Immediate Window** allows you to interact with the debugger by executing commands and evaluating expressions during a debugging session.

1. **How to Use the Immediate Window:**
   - To open the **Immediate Window**, go to **Debug > Windows > Immediate**.
   - In this window, you can evaluate expressions and modify variables on the fly.
2. **Practical Example:**
   - While debugging, if you want to change the value of `result`, you can type `result = 10` in the Immediate Window, and the change will take effect immediately without needing to modify the source code.

Call Stack

The **Call Stack** shows the order of function calls that led to the current point in the program's execution. It's helpful for tracing how a particular piece of code was reached.

1. **How to Use the Call Stack:**
   - To view the call stack, open **Debug > Windows > Call Stack**.
   - The call stack displays the functions that were called to reach the current line. You can click on any function in the call stack to navigate to it.
2. **Practical Example:**
   - If you are debugging a complex application and want to understand how a particular method

was reached, you can use the call stack to trace the method calls.

2. Best Practices for Troubleshooting

Debugging is not just about using tools—it's about having the right mindset and strategies for identifying and resolving issues effectively. Here are some best practices for troubleshooting in C#:

1. Break Down the Problem

Before diving into debugging, take a moment to break down the issue:

- **What is the symptom?** Is the application crashing, or is a feature not working as expected?
- **Where did it occur?** Try to narrow down the part of the application where the issue is happening (e.g., is it in a specific function or class?).
- **What changed recently?** If the problem didn't exist earlier, consider what was modified recently (code changes, data changes, configuration updates).

2. Use Meaningful Variable Names

One of the most effective ways to avoid bugs is to write clear, understandable code. Use descriptive variable and method names that reflect their purpose. This makes debugging much easier because you can more easily identify where something might be going wrong.

3. Test with Realistic Data

When debugging, use realistic data to test the application. If you only use simplified or dummy data, it's harder to identify edge cases or issues that may arise under real conditions.

4. Start with the Simple Checks

When an issue arises, start by checking the most common problems:

- Is the data being passed correctly?
- Are variables being initialized properly?
- Are there any typos or syntax errors?

Often, the issue is simpler than it appears, and you can resolve it by checking the basics.

5. Use Log Statements

In cases where debugging tools alone aren't enough, adding **log statements** to your code can help track down issues. You can log key variable values, execution paths, and error messages to a file or console to see what's happening in real-time.

3. Hands-On Project: Debugging an Application

Project Overview

For this hands-on project, we'll create a simple **to-do list application** that contains intentional bugs. Your task will be to use Visual Studio's debugging tools to identify and fix these bugs.

Here's the code for the **ToDoApp** class with intentional bugs:

csharp

```csharp
public class ToDoApp
{
    private List<string> tasks;

    public ToDoApp()
    {
        tasks = new List<string>();
    }

    public void AddTask(string task)
    {
        tasks.Add(task);
    }

    public string GetTask(int index)
    {
        return tasks[index];   // Bug: No bounds
checking for index
    }

    public void RemoveTask(string task)
    {
        tasks.Remove(task);
        tasks.RemoveAt(0);   // Bug: Always removes
the first task, not the specified one
    }

    public void DisplayTasks()
    {
        foreach (var task in tasks)
        {
            Console.WriteLine(task);   // Bug: Tasks
are not properly displayed in order
        }
    }
}
```

Step 1: Set Up the Debugging Environment

1. Open **Visual Studio** and create a new C# Console Application project.
2. and paste the above code into your project.

Step 2: Set Breakpoints

Set breakpoints at the following lines:

- Inside the `AddTask` method (to check the tasks being added).
- Inside the `RemoveTask` method (to check how tasks are being removed).
- Inside the `DisplayTasks` method (to inspect how tasks are displayed).

Step 3: Run the Application with Debugging

Run the application in debug mode by pressing **F5** or selecting **Debug > Start Debugging**. As the code runs, the debugger will pause at the breakpoints you set.

1. Inspect the values of variables, such as `tasks`, at each breakpoint.
2. Step through the code to see how the bugs manifest in real-time.

Step 4: Fix the Bugs

Bug 1: Index Out of Range Exception in `GetTask`

In the `GetTask` method, we are not checking if the index is within the bounds of the list before trying to access it. To fix this, add a bounds check:

```
csharp

public string GetTask(int index)
{
    if (index >= 0 && index < tasks.Count)
    {
        return tasks[index];
    }
    return "Invalid Task Index";   // Error message if
index is out of range
}
```

Bug 2: Always Removing the First Task in RemoveTask

In the RemoveTask method, we are always removing the first task in the list, regardless of which task was specified. To fix this, remove the specified task:

```
csharp

public void RemoveTask(string task)
{
    tasks.Remove(task);   // Remove the task correctly
}
```

Bug 3: Tasks Not Displayed Properly in DisplayTasks

In the DisplayTasks method, the tasks are not displayed in order because the list is being modified during display. To fix this, remove any modifications to the list inside the DisplayTasks method:

```
csharp

public void DisplayTasks()
{
    foreach (var task in tasks)
    {
        Console.WriteLine(task);   // Properly display
tasks in order
    }
}
```

Step 5: Run the Application Again

After fixing the bugs, run the application again in **Debug Mode** and test the functionality. The tasks should now be added correctly, removed properly, and displayed in the right order.

---

4. Real-World Applications of Debugging and Troubleshooting

Customer Support Systems

In customer support systems, debugging helps to identify issues that arise from user interactions, such as slow response times or errors when fetching data from a database. Developers use debugging tools to investigate the root cause of these problems and implement solutions quickly, ensuring that customers have a smooth experience.

Healthcare Applications

In healthcare applications, debugging is crucial for ensuring the integrity of patient data and the accuracy of medical calculations. For instance, a bug in medication dosages or patient history could have serious consequences. Debugging tools allow developers to pinpoint issues and resolve them before they affect patients.

Logistics and Inventory Systems

In logistics applications, real-time data handling is crucial. Debugging helps developers identify issues in data synchronization between warehouses, tracking systems, and inventory databases. It ensures that the system provides accurate and timely data to all stakeholders.

Conclusion

In this chapter, we explored **debugging** and **troubleshooting** in C#, focusing on the powerful debugging tools available in **Visual Studio**. We learned how to use **breakpoints, watches**, the **Immediate Window**, and the **Call Stack** to track down and fix issues in code.

We also walked through a hands-on project, where we debugged a simple **to-do list application** with intentional bugs and used Visual Studio's tools to identify and fix the problems.

By following the best practices for debugging and troubleshooting, you will be able to diagnose issues in your code more efficiently and write more reliable applications. In the next chapter, we will dive into **unit testing** and how to automate the process of verifying the correctness of your code, further improving your debugging workflow.

Happy debugging, and keep coding!

Chapter 15: Deploying C# Applications

Introduction to Deploying C# Applications

Deploying an application is the final step in the software development lifecycle. It's the process of making the application available for use by end-users, whether they are accessing it through a cloud service or running it as a standalone application on their machines. As a C# developer, knowing how to deploy your applications efficiently is crucial for delivering reliable and performant software to production environments.

In this chapter, we will explore how to deploy C# applications in two major ways:

1. **Deploying to the cloud**, specifically using **Microsoft Azure**.
2. **Deploying standalone executables** for desktop applications.

Additionally, we will walk through a hands-on project where we will deploy a simple **.NET Core web application** to Microsoft Azure and monitor its performance.

By the end of this chapter, you'll have the skills to deploy your applications to production environments, ensuring they are accessible, secure, and efficient.

What You'll Need

Software Requirements:

1. **Visual Studio**:
   - Visual Studio is the primary IDE used for C# development. It offers integrated tools for developing, testing, and deploying applications.
   - **Download**: You can download **Visual Studio Community Edition** from Visual Studio's website.

2. **Microsoft Azure**:
   - Azure is a cloud computing platform provided by Microsoft. It allows you to deploy, manage, and scale applications using various services like **App Services**, **Virtual Machines**, and **Azure SQL Database**.
   - **Create an Azure Account**: Go to Microsoft Azure and create a free account.

3. **.NET SDK**:
   - The **.NET SDK** is required to build and run your .NET applications.
   - **Download**: You can download the .NET SDK from Microsoft's .NET download page.

4. **Git** (for version control):
   - Git is essential for managing your code and collaborating with other developers.
   - **Download**: You can download Git from Git's official website.

5. **Azure CLI**:
   - The **Azure Command-Line Interface (CLI)** is a tool used to manage Azure resources directly from the terminal.

    o **Download**: Install it from Azure CLI.

Hardware Requirements:

- A **laptop or desktop** with **4GB of RAM** and **10GB of available disk space** is recommended for smooth performance during the development and deployment process.

Prerequisites:

- **Basic C# Knowledge**: Familiarity with C# and .NET Core is essential for this chapter.
- **Basic Web Development Knowledge**: A basic understanding of how web applications work (e.g., HTTP requests, web servers) will be useful.
- **Cloud Concepts**: Familiarity with cloud computing concepts like virtual machines, web apps, and databases will be helpful, but we will guide you through the cloud deployment process step by step.

Chapter Overview

In this chapter, we will:

1. **Understand Deployment Options**: Learn the different methods available for deploying C# applications, including cloud-based and standalone deployments.
2. **Deploying to Microsoft Azure**: Set up and deploy a .NET Core web application to Microsoft Azure, and monitor its performance.

3. **Deploying Standalone Executables**: Learn how to deploy .NET Core desktop applications as standalone executables.
4. **Real-World Application**: Explore how deployment fits into the larger software development lifecycle and its significance in business-critical applications like finance, healthcare, and logistics.

1. Understanding Deployment Options

Deployment refers to making your application available for use by end-users. There are multiple ways to deploy applications depending on the type of software you are building and the platform on which it will run. Below are the two primary deployment methods that we will cover in this chapter:

1.1 Deploying to the Cloud (Microsoft Azure)

Cloud deployment involves hosting your application on cloud platforms like **Microsoft Azure, Amazon Web Services (AWS)**, or **Google Cloud Platform (GCP)**. Cloud platforms offer several benefits:

- **Scalability**: Easily scale your application to handle increased traffic without manually provisioning more hardware.
- **Reliability**: Cloud providers offer redundancy and backups to ensure your application remains available even during hardware failures.
- **Global Access**: With cloud hosting, your application can be accessed by users around the world with low latency.

Why Choose Azure?

- **Integrated Services**: Azure integrates seamlessly with other Microsoft tools, making it a natural choice for C# developers.
- **Ease of Use**: Azure provides easy-to-use interfaces and templates for deploying C# applications.
- **Cost-Effective**: Azure provides a pay-as-you-go pricing model, making it affordable for small businesses and startups.

1.2 Deploying as Standalone Executables

For desktop applications, you might prefer deploying your application as a **standalone executable**. This method involves packaging your C# application into an executable (.exe) file that can be run on any Windows machine without requiring additional installations.

This is ideal for applications that don't require an internet connection or cloud infrastructure and need to run locally on user machines.

Why Choose Standalone Executables?

- **Offline Functionality**: Standalone applications can be run without an internet connection.
- **Simplicity**: They are easy to distribute, especially for smaller applications.

2. Deploying to Microsoft Azure

2.1 Setting Up Your Azure Environment

Before deploying your application, you need to create an **Azure account** and set up the necessary resources to host your app.

1. **Create an Azure Account:**
   - Visit the Azure website and sign up for a free account. The free tier provides access to various services like **App Services, Azure SQL Database,** and **Azure Blob Storage.**
2. **Set Up a Resource Group:**
   - In Azure, resources are grouped into **resource groups**. A resource group is a container for all the resources related to a specific application.
   - You can create a resource group by navigating to the **Azure Portal**, clicking **Create a Resource**, and selecting **Resource Group**.
3. **Set Up an Azure App Service:**
   - **App Services** are cloud-based platforms used to host web applications, APIs, and mobile backends.
   - In the **Azure Portal**, create a new **App Service** for hosting your .NET Core web application.
   - Select **Web App** under the **Create a Resource** menu.
   - Choose a **region, subscription,** and **resource group**.
   - Choose **.NET Core** as the runtime stack.

2.2 Preparing Your Application for Deployment

Now that your Azure environment is set up, let's prepare your **.NET Core web application** for deployment.

1. **Create a .NET Core Web Application**:
   - Open **Visual Studio**, create a new **ASP.NET Core Web Application** project, and select the **Web Application (Model-View-Controller)** template.
   - Here's a simple example of a HomeController in a web app:

```csharp
public class HomeController : Controller
{
    public IActionResult Index()
    {
        ViewData["Message"] = "Welcome to the Azure deployed application!";
        return View();
    }
}
```

2. **Publish the Application**:
   - In **Visual Studio,** right-click your project and select **Publish.**
   - Choose **Azure** as the target and follow the prompts to select your **App Service** created earlier.
   - Visual Studio will automatically handle the deployment process, including building the app and uploading it to Azure.

2.3 Monitoring and Scaling Your Application

After deploying the application, you can monitor its performance and scale it as needed.

1. **Azure Portal:**
   - Once your app is deployed, you can manage it directly from the **Azure Portal.** You can view metrics like **CPU usage, response times,** and **requests per minute.**
2. **Scaling:**
   - Azure allows you to **scale** your application vertically (by increasing resources like CPU and memory) or horizontally (by adding more instances of your app to handle higher traffic).
   - To scale, go to your **App Service** in the Azure Portal and select **Scale Up** or **Scale Out** depending on your needs.

---

3. Deploying Standalone Executables

For desktop applications, the process is different. You will build a **self-contained executable** that can run independently of any frameworks or runtimes.

3.1 Publish as Standalone Executable

.NET Core allows you to publish applications as standalone executables for Windows, macOS, and Linux. Here's how you can do it:

1. **Create a Console Application:**

- Open **Visual Studio** and create a new **Console App** project.

```csharp
using System;

class Program
{
    static void Main(string[] args)
    {
        Console.WriteLine("Welcome to the Standalone C# Application!");
    }
}
```

2. **Publish the Application**:
   - In **Visual Studio**, right-click your project and select **Publish**.
   - Choose **Folder** as the target and click **Publish**. This will generate a folder with your app's executable and all the necessary dependencies.
3. **Create a Self-Contained Executable**:
   - To create a self-contained executable, you can publish the app from the command line using the following command:

```bash
dotnet publish -c Release -r win-x64 --self-contained
```

This command tells .NET to create a Windows executable that includes all necessary dependencies for running the app on any machine, even if .NET Core is not installed.

4. Real-World Application: Deploying Business-Critical Applications

Finance

In the finance industry, applications need to be **highly available** and **secure**. **Cloud deployment** is often the best solution, as it provides redundancy, scalability, and security. A **real-time stock trading app** can benefit from **Azure App Services** for scalable web hosting, while **Azure SQL Database** can be used for secure and high-performance data storage.

Healthcare

Healthcare applications often need to store sensitive data, such as patient records, securely. **Cloud services** like **Azure** can offer compliance with healthcare regulations (such as **HIPAA** in the U.S.) while providing flexibility and scalability. **NoSQL databases** like **Cosmos DB** can be used for flexible data storage, while **Azure Monitor** can be used to monitor the application's performance.

Logistics

Logistics applications need real-time tracking and data synchronization. For example, a **fleet management system** can be deployed to **Azure** to track delivery trucks, monitor fuel consumption, and predict delivery times. The app can integrate with **Azure IoT Hub** to receive real-time data from connected devices in the trucks.

Conclusion

In this chapter, we covered the essentials of **deploying C# applications** to production environments. You learned how to deploy a **.NET Core web application** to **Microsoft Azure**, how to publish **standalone executables**, and the best practices for deploying business-critical applications in industries like **finance**, **healthcare**, and **logistics**.

Understanding how to deploy your applications is essential for delivering them to end-users and ensuring that they are reliable, scalable, and performant. In the next chapter, we will explore **advanced deployment strategies**, such as continuous integration (CI), continuous delivery (CD), and containerization, to help you deploy applications in an automated and efficient manner.

Happy deploying, and keep building!

www.ingramcontent.com/pod-product-compliance
Lightning Source LLC
LaVergne TN
LVHW022343060326
832902LV00022B/4212